A Touch of Larceny:

The Insurance Agent's Survival Guide

Kent P. Larsen

A Touch of Larseny:
The Insurance Agent's Survival Guide

Kent P. Larsen

Published by:

PUBLITEC Editions
273 Lower Cliff Drive
Post Office Box 4342
Laguna Beach, CA 92652

First printing 1984
Printed in U.S.A.

Library of Congress Catalog Card Number: 84-60877

Larsen, Kent P., 1937 -

A Touch of Larseny:
The Insurance Agent's Survival Guide

ISBN 0-913851-01-1

Dedicated to

all the men and women who left the insurance business thinking they were failures............

Preface

When I first offered this book to a friend for feedback, I was set back by his comments: "Kent, you wrote this from your intellect. Speak from the heart to these people who could learn so much from you. Speak the language of the heart."

Reading through the book again I saw a pattern in the thoughts I've shared with you, one I hadn't recognized before. As you read perhaps you'll see what I've seen.

My desire for simplicity, for ridding myself of distractions, for going directly to the best sources of learning the life insurance business ... the real goal of all these desires was to make myself fit for maximum service to my fellows and to my Creator as I understood him. This concept made me run: to sell a product that is of value to my fellows and which improves their quality of life by satisfying their need to show love for themselves and others.

If a man doesn't think he has value, why would he ever insure himself? To buy a million dollars worth of coverage he must feel like a million. He has to feel that his death would affect the lives of those he loves. If he refuses to protect them he must face these awful truths: that those so-called loved ones have value only if he is able to enjoy them; that when he stops everything stops; that he is a user, not a lover; that he is, in short, his own universe.

The process of building a trusting relationship with this man so that he could share his hopes, dreams, fears, and loves with me required my utmost concentration and effort. I had to learn how to listen and love. How could I spend time attending ego meetings, opening ego mail, and dealing with failures and mediocre managers when there were so many things to learn so that I could be of value to and trusted by my customers?

The games, contests, and other forms of manipulation by the agency and home office distracted me and pulled at my ego, taking me away from my true work: building others' self esteem so they'd want to insure it, and taking away their fear of becoming ill and losing their income (and their ability buy the props supporting their fragile self-images) by insuring that income.

The purpose of this book is to help you -- a salesperson who believes in a product, be it insurance, real estate, automobiles, or whatever -- to have the courage to hear your own music and to play it sweetly for the enjoyment and growth of others.

This is from my heart. Now read from my mind .....

First, special thanks go to the following special people:

C. Jerome Moore, Special Agent, Northwestern Mutual
for bringing me into this greatest of all business ventures.

Tom Goris, General Agent, Northwestern Mutual
who taught me how to block and tackle and held my hand those first years.

David James, Special Agent, Northwestern Mutual
who taught me the "business offer" presentation during my first two months in the business and has been my mentor and friend all these years.

Tom Otteson, Special Agent, Northwestern Mutual
whose splendid example kept me on the right track and warm friendship I still cherish.

Tom Thorkelson, Special Agent, Northwestern Mutual
for having the courage and integrity to tell me to stay with my company when I wanted to leave and go with him during my third year in the business.

David Roberson, General Agent, Penn Mutual
for praying with me at some of my darkest hours.

Millard Grauer, Past President, Million Dollar Round Table
for his love and counsel.

Frank Sullivan, President, Mutual Benefit
for being my friend unconditionally in good and bad times.

Gus, Walter, Noel, and Tom Hansch, General Agents, Mutual Benefit
for expanding my mind and encouraging personal freedom and creativity.

Northwestern Mutual
for teaching me the meaning of dedication and excellence.

Mutual Benefit
for teaching me the meaning of love and concern.

Ben Feldmen
for being himself and sharing it.

Contents

Something's Wrong 1

Simplify, Simplify 9

Agency Meetings 10
Home Office Conventions 12
After the Ball (the Convention) Was Over 19
Agency Bulletins 20
Contests 21
One Card Systems 23
Home Office Training Courses 24
Planning and Goal Setting 25
The Competition 27
Commissions 28
Renewals 29
CLU 30
Secretaries 33
Paperwork (Why Agents Think They Hate It) 35
Your Title -- Or, What You Do For a Living 37
Your Car and the Way You Dress 39
Your Office 40

Understanding Your Co-Workers 41

General Agents 42
A Note to General Agents 43
Home Office Officials 44
A Note to Home Office People 45
Underwriters 47
Technicians and Specialists 48
Brokerage Managers 49
Lawyers and Accountants 51
Big Hitters 53
Something For the "Old Pros" 54

Finding Your Customers 55

Prospecting 56
Who Do You Call On? Who Do You See? 57
After You've Chosen Your Industry 59

Taking It To the Street 61

What's Going to Motivate You to Sell? 62
Why People Don't Buy Life Insurance 66
Why People DO Buy Life Insurance 68
When They Say "No, I Don't Want to See You" 69
When They Say "No, I Don't Want to Buy" 70
When They Want to Cancel the Policy 72
Joint Work 74
Replacing Policies 75
Rated Cases 78
Kickbacks ("Consulting Fees") 80
Public Relations 83
What Do You Have to Sell? 84
Par or Non-Par? 87
Net Cost 88
Term Insurance 89
Some Tips on Selling Term Insurance 91

Building Relationships (and Your Business) 93

Recruiting 94
Fact Finders 96
The Medical 98
Newsletters and Monthly Mailings 100
Study Groups 101
What to Read and Study 102
Recommended Reading For You and Your Customers 103

So What Are You Going To Do Now? 105

Appendix: A Couple of Related Pieces 107

The Businessman -- Is He Really a Big Bad Wolf? 109
Just a Salesman (With David H. James, CLU) 115

Something's Wrong...

Few industries offer as much assistance and pay as much attention to new people as the life insurance industry does.

A person recruited into the business must pass through a battery of tests and interviews, all designed to point out any problem areas that might prevent that individual from being successful.

Next, the prospective agent is usually asked to do a "survey" wherein he or she contacts friends and asks them about their feelings concerning life insurance products.

Finally, the prospective agent is introduced to successful agents and invited to ask many questions. When he or she signs up, the new agent is often shipped out to the home office for training and education, with followup in the local agency.

Our new agent then begins a career, full of enthusiasm and armed to the teeth with products, sales tracks, and brochures. Product and people education continues in these early months and the agent is watched closely by the general agent or manager. Suggestions and help are offered and given all along the way.

The home office arranges awards and recognition for new agents and usually has a special division assigned to monitor their progress, complementing the local agency program.

Even with all this attention and assistance, only three or four agents out of a HUNDRED qualify for the independent sales organization known as the Million Dollar Round Table (MDRT). Each year only three or four percent of all agents sell enough to get above the poverty level in first year commissions.

In most cases, our new agent is out of the business within the year.

Why? What's wrong? Why such a high turnover? Why such low productivity?

Agents have 24 hours in a day. Everyone they meet is a potential customer. There are no strikes, no unions, no shortage of product, no capital requirements. Why can't an agent sell at least one $40,000 policy each week for about $35 a month in premium? Especially now in this inflationary economy when large amounts of life insurance are necessary to protect the family, the estate, the business?

To get a better picture, let's consider three agents. The first has been in the business for 18 months, the second 4 years, and the last 15 years. They have the same problem: they each need a sale .....

The Agent With 18 Months in the Business

You've been summoned to an 8:30 a.m. private meeting with your general agent. You stand outside the door ready to knock with your guts rolling .....

Three months have flown by. You haven't had a sale. You owe him a ton of money. Now, even if you do get a sale you're still in the hole. When you win the best you can do is tie .....

You've phonied up your sales reports listing how many people you called, how many you saw, how many fact-finding interviews you held, how many referred leads you got. Your inventory of people you hope to sell in the next 30 days is a nightmare of wishful thinking .....

You ask yourself what you did these past 90 days and nights. You got up, went down to the agency, pushed white cards, blue cards, and home office paperwork around ... attended Monday morning meetings ... went to three life underwriter meetings ... studied your CLU courses ... read every piece of mail sent to you .....

You listened to motivational tapes and when you finished one you reached for the phone and made a call ... and felt sick inside when the guy on the other end was nice ... but didn't want to see you .....

You walked down the agency corridors, sat for hours with top agents, told them you were doing fine, and listened to them tell you how great the business is .....

Your general agent smiled at you every day, made excuses for your failure to be in the weekly bulletin listing the submitted and paid for business of all the agents. He even stopped by your office and smiled reassuringly as he saw you feverishly filling out white cards and blue cards and putting them in nice neat rows in the gray box .....

Your direct mail bill for the quarter came in, telling you that over ten thousand mortgage leads were mailed in your name. There were four return post cards. You called each one of them ... one had cancer, another was already dead, another had had open heart surgery, and the last just wanted the free road map .....

Time just passed so quickly. You felt like you were working. You visited friends, you kept on the lookout for prospects, you asked people the right questions. You do have a few good prospects ... but here you are, so far in the hole financially and emotionally that you just can't see how you're ever going to get out of it .....

You wish the general agent would just tell you to clean out your desk, but you know he won't, not as long as there's any hope you'll pay him back. And even if you just walked out, that paper you signed said that all advances had to be repaid, at interest, and you remember hearing from ex-agents how they were hounded and their salaries attached until the debt was paid off .....

So here you are, so full of high expectations in the beginning and now so beaten by what you see as your failure ... and you have to reach up and knock on the general agent's door .....

He greets you with a warm smile and motions you to sit down. He comes out from behind the desk and sits in a chair opposite you. You notice how relaxed he is, how neatly dressed. You remember how impressed you were when he first showed you his personal records from his days as an agent 10 years ago ... all those numbers in the sales book, beautifully recorded, legible, always showing improvement month after month .....

You glance up at the three MDRT plaques on the wall, his CLU diploma, his degree from a midwestern university ... he was even an officer in the service. On his desk is a picture of his well-groomed wife and his three children, all smiling confidently at him .....

His personal planning book is on his desk for all the agents to see. He has his vacation time plotted, meetings at the home office scheduled, his study group dates noted. The financial section demonstrates how he gives his wife so much money each month ... and how she actually has some left for Christmas at the end of the year .....

His policies have no loans. He lives within his means. In addition to building the agency, he manages to write nearly a million of coverage on friends and old customers back in the midwest .....

You remember how he has a good, honest answer for just about every question concerning the business, your personal life, your career. His philosophy is letter perfect in its consistency. In short, you're certain that you have the very best agent ever born .....

But you haven't had a sale for nearly three months and you're scared to death .....

The meeting lasts an hour and a half. You pour your heart out. In the end he gives you a reassuring pat on the back, tells you "All you need is more activity" ... and sends you back out and down the road to your personal hell .....

The Agent With Four Years in the Business

You're at the Monday morning agency meeting. The tape recorder blares out the Marine Corps Hymn and John Phillip Sousa marches. Bleary eyed, you grope for the coffee pot and mumble hello's to your fellow agents .....

The meeting begins. The general agent strides up to the podium in the beautifully appointed general agency meeting room. He greets you with a bang of his fist pounding to the tempo of the march music. "Feel that spirit, people," he screams. "Damn it, this is a great business!"

His unit managers gather round and call out last week's production. Even a $2,500 juvenile policy written by a 58-year-old agent with 30 years in the business brings on a rousing cheer .....

Medals and awards are produced ... a visit to the agency by a home office official next week is announced ... next month's trip to Hawaii for the agent with the most disability income premium is discussed. (The company has a push on for disability premium this quarter. Otherwise they'll have to fire their one disability underwriter. He has nothing to do because the company never accepts any risks .....)

There's an overwhelming, almost suffocating, atmosphere of high-pitched enthusiasm. EVERYONE in the agency seems to have sold a policy last week ... except you ... you haven't had a sale in four weeks. And here you are four years in the business, once a "rising star" touted as a potential leader of the company .....

The sales idea of the week is described by a unit manager who heard of an agent who made 34 unsuccessful cold calls in an industrial unit. On the 35th attempt he walked in and said "Do any of you guys want any of this rotten insurance I'm selling?" and actually got an invitation to make a presentation .....

The sales idea of the month is offered by another unit manager who has produced a direct mail letter with a great sound to it. You clip a dollar bill to the letter and say that this is a taxfree dollar and that you have more to give the guy if he'll give you an appointment. There's an enthusiastic round of applause. Everyone vows to send 50 of these letters to attorneys and CPAs. Why not get their personal insurance with this great idea and referrals as well? .....

The meeting ends with a round of applause for the unit manager of the week. You try to get to the general agent as he leaves the room but your unit manager is in the way ... looking at you with knowing eyes. You turn, dump the coffee in the trash can, and leave .....

You walk down the corridor where the secretaries are reading the morning paper and chit-chatting while they wait for the agents to get back to work. You finally wind up in your office ... a corner unit with a 270-degree view ... knowing full well that next year you'll have to vacate for a bullpen desk and watch a new "rising star" take your place ... bring his wife, mother, father, and cousin up to see his new furniture ... and his new dream .....

And you haven't had a sale in weeks and don't think you'll ever get one again .....

The Agent With 15 Years in the Business

Your desk is piled with paperwork. Undelivered policies are stacked on the floor. Unopened mail is piled on the "customer" chair next to your desk. You are bored to death. Can't seem to do anything but shuffle one paper over to one side of the desk ... put the paper into a folder ... put the folder in a spot where it has top priority over all the other papers .....

Unanswered phone messages are punched onto the wire nail sticking out of the "Leader in Lives" award you received ten years ago. Magazines, articles, and tax news letters are off in the corner on the floor near the doorway. You vow that you'll take them home Friday to read over the weekend .....

Personal and business expense bills are lying in the middle of your desk. They're a month late. You have the money ... you just don't feel like writing checks .....

An old friend who was once a tough prospect calls at 10:30 and asks you to lunch. His wife finally found out about his affair with a supplier's secretary and wants to nail him to the wall ... he needs to talk to you .....

You go to lunch, listen to the guy spill his guts. You turn your shirt collar around, counsel him the best you can ... give him a hug when he leaves, half in the bag, and watch the poor guy stumble to his car .....

You're drained and your head hurts and it's now two in the afternoon. You go back to the office to the same pile of paper ... reach in the small refrigerator and take out a bottle of apricot brandy. It tastes good ... you let its warmth fill you up ... energy returns. You reach for the phone and start to answer those phone messages. While you're waiting on hold you start opening mail and throwing out the trash .....

Soon you're engaged in a conversation with another old customer with a problem. His father is really starting to fail. Could you come by the house this evening and talk to the old guy and convince him to make out a will? "Sure," you say, "that's what I'm here for" .....

At five you call home and listen to that sweet voice you love ... 23 years you've heard it and it's still wonderful. Your voice slurs a little and she asks if you've been drinking. "Oh, just a little, honey ... some wine at lunch with Elmer Electric" .....

As you put the phone down your general agent leans in the door and sighs .....

"I don't know what I'd do if you weren't here. Dealing with these young agents is getting tougher and tougher." You ask him in. He waves his hand "No" as you offer him some brandy ... and unloads. You're totally wiped out but you listen and care. The poor guy is in trouble ... if he didn't have your premium and a couple of the other old guys he'd be out the window. He'd be a better guy to have around if he'd just loosen up and have a beer once in a while, you think to yourself .....

You close up shop, wondering what you do for a living. Get in the car and turn on the FM ... too much static. Put in a Streisand tape ... ah, that's it. She sings "Funny Valentine" to you ... and big tears run down your face while you drive .....

The lights are on in the driveway. You go in ... to a different world ... a world you love. Your wife tells you that your general agent called, saying he was sorry to bother you at home but could you have a 7:30 breakfast tomorrow with him and a prospective agent? He says he knows that the young guy will be really impressed if you're there and he's just about to choose between your agency and another one uptown.

You agree, go to the refrigerator, take out a dill pickle and eat it before kissing your wife so she won't be overcome by the brandy .....

And you haven't had a sale in almost a month .....

****

What are these guys doing wrong? What is their problem?

These questions are impossible to answer because each agent is an individual ... no two are alike.

But, I DO think that I have some food for thought, and that's what this book is all about .....

Simplify, Simplify

What you're about to read has enraged many management folks. And, this section has prevented this book from being published by insurance industry publishers. (They don't make their money selling books to agents. They sell books to insurance companies who either give or resell them to agents.)

For those readers in management, I offer this:

If you feel anger, resentment, and hostility, check your thinking carefully. Anger is based in fear. What are you afraid of? Put yourself in the agent's position. Get out of yourself for a few minutes. Forget that you earn a living perpetuating mediocrity and failure, that the occasional successes are in SPITE of an ignorant philosophy of sales management and training.

Bet you're really hot now. Who is this smart aleck anyway? How dare he say such things?

How dare I?

Because I MADE it selling, my friend. Not sitting in the agency office, the district office, or the home office telling people how to sell. I did it ... and I did it in some very large numbers.

Listen to me. Take what you want and leave the rest. But please, listen to me. I mean you no harm. I'd like to help you grow, and growth for all of us is painful. Write down what you fear, write down your FEELINGS about what I'm saying as you read. There's magic in writing with pen and paper ... you'll learn so very much so very fast .....

Agency Meetings

The agency meeting is the biggest distraction and biggest money waster in the life insurance industry. The best agency meetings I've ever been to are the ones I skipped, going out and making sales instead.

One thing to remember: People in management love meetings. Unfortunately, agency meetings can be far more distracting and destructive than constructive, especially if you're not selling.

Don't attend more than one a month. If yours is a once-a-week or more type agency, take this practice as a great big red flag warning you to stay away. Once a month is all you need, and then only if the purpose of that meeting is to help you learn new selling skills and to bring you new ideas .....

One distracting thing about most agency meetings is that THEY try to tell you about all THEIR problems and how they're going to solve them. Like: "Folks, we finally have our correspondence volume under control. We're putting in a word processing machine next month so we can increase our office efficiency."

Or: "The home office has announced that they're now in the process of reviewing all policies with an eye toward re-vamping them and coming out with a whole new series to meet the competition." You'll be thinking about this great new product and forgetting that you already have a great old product and that nothing really significant has taken the place of whole life and yearly renewable and convertible term in the last 100 years or so. They scare you into thinking that there might be competition out there when you never seem to run into any .....

Another problem that comes up at agency meetings is that there's always some fellow agent with a gripe who's frustrated enough to bring it up and take a pot shot at management in front of the whole group. Since misery loves company, more agents join in. Later, long after the meeting is over, they're still discussing the topic. Hours and hours of discussion .....

You don't need this kind of distraction. You need a sale.

How do you get a sale? By being out with your people, people who can buy your product if you offer it to them properly after you've won their hearts and trust.

You don't get a sale at an agency meeting.

So what do you do when meetings are scheduled? Without making yourself conspicuous, just stay away most of the time. Don't worry about no one being there ... there will always be agents attending agency meetings .....

Want to know how can you have a really great agency meeting? Organize a softball game on Sunday with games and prizes for all the kids, big and small. No home office literature or announcements. No technical stuff. Just fun and enjoyment with guys and gals who have mutual problems.

Agency meetings should be one-on-one meetings between agent and manager or in small controlled groups with specific sales-oriented goals.

One a month ... and that's probably too many.

Home Office Conventions

I want to tell you a story about what I experienced at a typical home office convention. And then I want you to forget it.

I've included this story in this book because I feel it's important for you and I to relate to each other, for you to know that we've experienced some of the same thoughts .....

So read this story of a home office convention and feel my frustration and loneliness and then I'll tell you another story .....

You get off the plane, take a taxi to the hotel, and walk in the lobby on registration day.

Home office people are all over the place, greeting you with smiles and chatter. You register at the hotel counter and then go to the mezzanine where the folding tables are loaded with the latest home office news. Two tables contain boxes holding large manilla envelopes, each with an agent's name on it. A dippy looking dish who hates being there is madly searching for a big hitter's envelope .....

You can tell he's a big hitter. He has stripes on his tennis shorts ... he's wearing sandals that show his ugly feet ... he has on a tee-shirt with the company logo blasting at you ... his fat belly is sticking out ... he's puffing on a foot-long cigar. He yells at the poor frustrated girl that his envelope "MUST be there! DO YOU KNOW WHO I AM?"

Other agents start rooting around in the boxes for their envelopes and the girl screams at them to stop. A general agent runs up, demands the girl's name, and runs off again .....

A young agent and his wife stand patiently in line watching with wide eyes. This is their first convention. He sold his grandmother $200,000 of term on the last day of qualification and just made his quota ... paid the premium with their "egg money" .....

"Big Hitter" finds his envelope. (It was filed under "Big" rather than "Hitter.") He walks a few feet away from the table, ripping the envelope open. Suddenly a scream of rage fills the room. Like a mad bull Big Hitter charges up to the table waving his plastic name tag. "Where's my MDRT ribbon? Where's my 100 Lives Club ribbon? How come I have a white name tag? It should be green to show that I have over 25 million in force!!"

The whole place is in an uproar. The home office vice president in charge of home office conventions runs up ... he's waving a staple gun and has a thousand multi-colored ribbons and badges bulging out of every pocket. He throws his arms around Big Hitter and weeps with him while they change the name tag and staple on the ribbons. Agents who didn't earn ribbons crowd close so they can steal some and tack them onto their badges ....

Exhausted by this struggle, you go up to your room carrying your own bags because you don't want to tip anyone ... you haven't sold much but you DID qualify ... and there'll be a free meal and cocktail hour in about 30 minutes .....

You change clothes and hustle your wife along to the mini-ballroom where the cocktail hour and buffet are going on. "Is my badge straight, honey? Do I look successful?" .....

As you walk the corridor leading to the entrance you spot the company president, vice president, and director of agencies shaking hands with the agents and their wives as they come in. What a thrill! You and your wife are about to shake hands with men who control BILLIONS OF DOLLARS OF ASSETS! Men who LOVE you ... (men who hate your guts because you're the biggest pain in the whole system) ... men who will soon mount the small stage to welcome you to the convention and tell you how wonderful it is to have you all there .....

The executive officers' wives get quietly smashed off in the corner, trying desperately to avoid all the general agents' wives ... they absolutely cringe when their husbands come over with a general agent in tow .....

If you're lucky you squeeze your way to the bar and get a couple of drinks and find the white saucer-sized dishes and toothpicks stacked around the single long table in the center of the room holding all the goodies. You push, shove, and fight for the last shrimp ... and then try to hold a place in line until the waiters bring another tray. (Two waiters are serving the entire bunch. After all, hold the line on expenses. Remember that all this is coming right out of the policy holder's pocketbook) .....

After the president gives his brief, phoney welcome amid the wild cheers of the "faithful," the lights blink off and on, signalling you to start leaving. And off you go, up to your room for fear that someone will invite you down to the bar where drinks are $2.50 each. Because you look successful and sold three million last year (only $18,000 of premium) you'd be expected to throw some dough around. And since you're rather new to the

---

company, other agents want to check you out, to see if you're material for their study group ... and you don't feel up to being "looked over" .....

The first morning of the convention finds you in the main ballroom. A brass band blares out as pretty young things in cheerleader garb dance on the stage. Everyone is hung over ... some of the wives have to be carried in.

The only ones early are the agents in the front row who are going to be introduced as "stars" ... "your leaders." They're in splendid shape ... eager ... smiling ... looking back at the people coming in ... yelling and waving ... happy guys you hate instantly .....

Your wife senses your frustration as you look toward the front rows. She pats your hand and says "Honey, you can do it ... next year you'll be up there." You want to hit her right in the mouth .....

The band stops ... lights out ... spotlight on ... ladies and gentlemen, I give you your president, BERGY BUDGET! The band blares ... all rise and clap ... tears begin to form in the president's eyes ... he waits, nods grandly, and then with great supplication pleads with you to stop ... but all the home office people scattered throughout the audience just will not stop ... they know that Bergy Budget stands for everything they hold dear, including, and most importantly:

> Screw the Agent
> Whenever,
> Wherever, and
> However You Can.

Finally the applause stops. Bergy Budget starts with a welcome, asks for slides, and begins to point out the growth of the company since the mid-1800's. Percentage points, numbers, and statistics leap from his frothing lips ... especially when the investment return slide appears. There's a tremor in his voice ... no, it cracks ... he caresses the numbers as they pour out.

And then on to operating expenses. His voice becomes severe. He shows the problem: TOO MUCH NEW BUSINESS! You agents are breaking us. We have all the insurance in force we will ever want and you still bring us more! Don't you realize you how much it costs us to put new policies in force? Don't you know that the greatest risk to the company is during a policy's first two years? I'll show you!

Medical Director! I don't want policies issued to anyone who could possibly die. I only want people who will live forever and who will never borrow on their policies. Insurance Vice President! Make these policies so hard to get that no one will even DARE TRY! Cut the commission schedule! No more production bonus commissions! And if any policy holder borrows on his cash values, get the agent in here and tell him to get in line! This is MY COMPANY AND MY MONEY! Take his persistency bonus away! THAT will teach him not to let policy holders borrow!

Bergy Budget is rolling, cheered on by the home office people and the general agents waiting for a bigger agency.

Suddenly, he shuts off the projector with a click of his handheld control. He turns ... lights are dimmed ... a single spotlight falls on his face ... the audience is hushed ... and Bergy Budget speaks in soft, affectionate tones .....

"You people are the finest bunch of agents in the industry. Over half of you are now CLUs ... over a third of you are MDRT ... the top 100 agents in the company produced more business than all but 15 life companies. You are responsible for our growth and success by constantly bringing us quality policy holders, those who promise not to die and who don't borrow, year after year. I want to tell you how much I appreciate the way you've responded to our request to cut policy loans ... and if you don't continue to respond I remind all of you that it takes 14 years to be vested and I'll cancel your contracts if you don't cooperate!"

A roar of applause ... feet are stamping ... Yes! Yes! they cry ... cut out commissions for the good of the policy holder! Deny insurance to those who might die! We're with you, Bergy Budget! Hooray! Death to agents with policy loans exceeding the company average! Upward! Onward!

Now the company leaders are introduced. One by one they are paraded up on the stage with a cute comment. Pictures of their families are flashed on the screen. They are asked to make a three-minute speech ... each one humbly admits that without this glorious company and his general agent's constant attention, he'd never be up there looking down on all you folks .....

Next, a speech from the director of agencies. More love ... more praise ... the general agents go wild as they cheer him on. Each one has been up all night trying to get next to him and get the inside track on the big metropolitan agency that's coming up for grabs .....

On with the show. Each general agent has made certain that his "stars" are on the afternoon program. The clique must be served. Content, sales ideas, and quality presentation take a back seat to star status and the general agents' egos. You sit through hour after hour of talks on "How to Prospect," "The Professional Market," "How I Stopped Drinking and Got Religion When My General Agent Extended My Loan" ... and on and on and on .....

Out of the whole mess you're lucky to come away with one idea ... that is, if you don't fall asleep .....

It's the second and last afternoon of the convention. Your wife is sick from the spoiled chicken salad served at the wives' luncheon. She's also fed up with the gossip, the questions, the answers ... she's there only because you're there. The general agent's wife was supposedly going to "mother" the new wives but she's been too busy paying homage to the big wigs or mingling with the other general agents' wives and talking about all the crap her husband has to take from those jerks .....

The meeting ends the way it began. Bergy Budget makes a final speech and hopes to see you all back next year. He reminds you that checkout time is noon ... it's 1:30 when his speech ends ...

Your bag is packed and in the lobby. You say goodbye to the folks you hung around with, the same folks you'll be seeing tomorrow, the folks in your agency. You hung around with them out of a need to feel comfortable. No one else even talked to you ... they only talked to big hitters. You didn't have the right ribbons ... you had a white new-guy name card and you had too much integrity to steal a ribbon .....

So back to the airport. You go home ... you're depressed and don't know why ... your bags are loaded with copies of the speeches and presentations that you'll never look at again ... you missed two days' work ... spent $50 you shouldn't have ... had three fights with your wife ... and you want to quit the business .....

But you can't quit. You owe money. You've sold some policies and you like the money ... you like the work ... you just don't know if you can do it again .....

******

You can. Especially if you never attend another company convention. Stay away from them. Some people say you meet great folks ... true, but can you sell them a policy?

The only convention you attend is MDRT ... and an occasional local underwriter's meeting if they have a really great speaker and not some guy from your area whose general agent is trying to promote .....

Just go out and see people. Things will work out ... and you won't miss two days of production and another three because you're depressed ... and your wife won't get sick on the rotten chicken salad .....

After the Ball (the Convention) Was Over

When I wrote that story, I reached back in my memory bank, pulled it out, and wrote it exactly as I felt.

What's missing in the story is the fact that my dearest friends, David James, Tom Otteson, Steve Peskoff, and Ed Tippets also attended that convention from different cities and I met them there ... and we became life-long friends.

You see, probably like you, I went to home office conventions with false hopes, filled with false expectations. Hoping to go "home" ... yearning to be "filled with the spirit" ... looking and searching for something that wasn't there and never will be. Only by the grace of God did I find what was important ... friends from all over the country.

Go to the home office convention for one purpose only ... to find fellow agents who will become close friends. But not too close ... the geographical barrier is important because it lets you build the "perfect relationship." You're together for only a few days so you see them at their best and they see you at your best. You don't know their sins and they don't know yours.

As far as gaining any new knowledge? New ideas? You will ... from those friends, rarely from any program put on by corporate people trying to be salespeople for a one-week stand.

Applaud the obvious propaganda with the secret understanding that home office people need to think that their company is the VERY BEST. We know that the VERY BEST company is the company on the risk when someone dies, the company that issued the policy. But don't tell them that ... you can destroy months of pep talks by supervisors.

Be nice to home office people. You are a guest in THEIR house. But be certain to find those very valuable "not too close" friends you'll enjoy all your life.

Agency Bulletins

Agency bulletins scare me to death. They come in the mail each month like messengers of a great big secret, bringing silent fear.

Oh, how I wish they'd disappear.

I feel like screaming at the general agent that he has no right to publish my production. That he doesn't publish HIS production bonus commissions. That no one has a right to know what I produce. That it's none of my business what anyone else produces. To take my name out. To leave me alone. To give me some peace. To let me sink in my own mediocrity.

But there they are for the whole world to see.

They drive me nuts ... except when I've had a great month and a great year. How I love them then! I search the mail, eager to see my name on top. I look at those beautiful numbers over and over again .....

And then the slump ... the growing time ... the tired time ... the weeks that go by without a sale. No numbers appear. I hide out ... stay away from other agents.

Folks out there in sales land, I don't know if these pieces of paper listing our records are good or bad. I suspect they're a little of both.

Depending on your self-image, your honesty with yourself, and your willingness to accept responsibility for your actions, agency bulletins can be constructive and inspiring ... or they can put you out of the business.

I guess it depends on your attitude. You can watch other agents successfully dealing with each day, building their businesses, all with the same problems you have. Their success can give you hope and a willingness to grow and take the pain that personal growth seems to thrive on. And, if you care for others, there are special rewards in watching how the rookies do and the old guys too, and maybe saying a kind word of encouragement to someone on the bottom of the list.

I'd like to forget the foolish things I've done just to have my name up in lights on the bulletin. But then, they were all learning experiences. They taught me that shortcuts don't bring satisfaction, that when I pulled those deals and saw my name on top when I opened the bulletin, there was no joy.

Contests

If you don't know how to handle them, contests can cut you to ribbons and put you out of the business.

The minute a contest is announced you have to gear up your brain and re-think your reasons for being in this business and what it is that's going to make you successful.

Far too often, a contest makes you feel sort of unclean, as if you're going to go out and "nail" every innocent soul you meet to win or at least make a respectable showing. So you hate contests. You bad mouth the agency manager and tell everyone that you think contests are dumb and demeaning and that you're beyond such childish manipulations. After all, you're a PROFESSIONAL.

A few days into the thing, you see other agents turning in applications and making you look bad in your own eyes. You really don't want to compete with anyone. You really don't want to measure your performance with the others'. You really want to be left alone and not put into a fishbowl. The agency bulletin is bad enough ... do they have to beat you to death with another contest too?

As the weeks pass, you get angry, don't you? Sure! And then it happens ... you get hot, red hot, and you DO go out and nail everyone you meet. You DO go out and take applications just to take them. You DO push your good customers around a bit and think of all kinds of quick schemes to get them to buy another policy.

In short, you start doing all the things you shouldn't be doing. You pay the first month's premium. You roll a guy over into a new policy and let the old one float on the values that exist. You make a presentation based on how it's going to affect your stats and not on what the customer wants or needs.

You go home frustrated and if you win you feel that everyone resents you. If you lose you resent "Mr. Clean" and his smiling wife at the awards dinner and vow never again to participate in a contest.

It seems to me that before every contest, the agency manager should call a meeting, not only to explain the rules and awards, but to reinforce certain values and put things in proper perspective .....

"Folks, this contest is goint to be a grand affair and I want you to keep doing all the things you've been doing, but for this short period of time I want you to do more of them. To reach out and put more into this emotional business. To energize yourself for a short burst of concentrated activity. I want you to polish your skills and close more often.

"Keep the customers' best interests at heart but have the courage to force them to a decision for their own benefit. Know that you have not only their needs at heart but that you have an additional personal incentive to see what you can do when you really put things together.

"So keep this contest in perspective. Don't chase a sale just to place high in the standings. Even though you'll undoubtedly hear or actually see other agents pumping in business just to make them look good, business that will never be paid for, remember that their achievements will be hollow."

If the general agent or manager would see to it that this sort of pep talk were given at EVERY contest announcement and at various points during the contest, honest hardworking agents would benefit and so would the customer.

And, when you did your best for this very short period of time, it would give you peace of mind and confidence. You'd know that you can pull yourself up and out of any financial hole you may dig yourself into if you just put things together and push.

Contests should be fun. They should generate excitement and help everyone grow. And they can, if you keep them in proper perspective.

One Card Systems

If it's called a one card system, why are there so many cards?

In nearly any other setting, a grown person seen cutting the tabs off pink, red, blue, green, yellow, and white cards would be sent to the funny farm.

What are you dealing with? Cards or people? Do you want to translate warm, wonderful people you learn to love into cards?

If you want a one card system, have one ... on one card. Take an index card and write down the names of a bunch of people you'd like to see about an idea. Then go see them.

And don't cross them off the card as you see them. They are people with their own value systems, loves, hopes, and hates. If they don't buy your idea, don't "cross them off"; make a check mark instead. Drawing a line through someone's name is like killing them or saying they don't count. If your kid doesn't buy your ideas on premarital sex, do you cross him off your list?

You've sold policies to a lot of people or you're going to sell policies to a lot of people and you need a system for keeping track of them.

What's wrong with your commission statement prepared by the home office? It tells you when the renewal commission is paid, and that's the anniversary of the policy. Too simple?

Age change? Do you actually think that people are motivated to buy life insurance because their age is changing? They buy because they have a problem and they trust you and know that you care.

Sit back and reflect a moment. Did you buy YOUR policy because of an age change? Or was it a contest?

Home Office Training Courses

... were written by home office people. That should be reason enough to be suspicious of their value. If the course tries to take you beyond the rate book, the application, and basic underwriting, approach it with caution.

Most of the home office training courses I've seen were written by folks who couldn't make it selling, by attorneys who couldn't make it on their own and who own a $15,000 decreasing term and have 15 kids, or by people who couldn't even make it as managers.

As a result, you get a very logical and professional technique that would give R2D2 fits.

What we get from these courses is a boring, laborious attempt to teach the buyer all he ever wanted to know about life insurance and was afraid to ask for fear an agent would try and tell him.

Instead of just asking "Who would be hurt, who would cry tonight, if you died today?" they want you to put on demonstrations with charts, line graphs, tables, and "put a fence around your fortune" red letter language.

Remember, life insurance is already sold. It was sold years and years ago. Nobody has to be sold on the value of life insurance. If I asked you if you'd take another $100,000 of coverage, would I have to tell you all about its value? Heck no. You'd just want to know what it costs. That's all. What does it cost?

And just what DOES it cost? Volumes have been written about that one simple question. Debates rage in home office think tanks all over the country. Listen:

A policy costs the first year's premium. It's $4,000 if you want to own it and $1,000 if you want to rent it. What do you want? Are you a renter or a buyer?

End of subject.

(Oh, dear ... 50,000 technicians and professionals at the home office just got canned. And you just picked up hours and hours for seeing people and asking them who they love most .....)

Planning and Goal Setting

Once each year in most agencies, there's a time set aside for annual reviews. During these days the general agent is guarded by his staff who speak in hushed, almost religious tones. "Mr. GA? Ssssssh, please. I just cannot disturb him until next week. It's ANNUAL REVIEW TIME!" Candles are lit and placed next to his door. When the GA does appear he is serious, drawn, and perhaps in need of a haircut and shave. These are trying times for a general agent. The home office has asked for a composite report of what his office will produce and they want it in BLOOD!

Are you not somewhat in awe, Ms. or Mr. Agent? You should be. What you put down on your annual review form for lives, premium, and volume is about to become the basis of a MULTI-BILLION DOLLAR COMPANY'S corporate plan! Is it any wonder that so much has been written on planning and goal setting?

Actually, this is one of the more violent forms of distraction the business offers. Violent because if you don't meet your goals the general agent can get quite nasty.

Questions on forms given to me over the years are listed below along with recommended answers in keeping with the intelligence behind the questions.

1. If you had only six months to live, what would you do?
   Scream and cry.

2. Regardless of money, skill, or talent, if you could do anything in life, what would you do?
   Play all day, every day.

3. How much premium do you need this year?
   More than last year.

4. How many lives will you do this year?
   One for each policy.

5. How much volume will you do this year?
   If the minimum policy is $2,500, at least that much on each policy.

6. What are your three most important goals for next year?
   To obtain air, water, and food.

---

7. If you had to leave the business this year, what would you do?
I'm not leaving this year.

How quickly I was able to fill out the form each year. Once I wrote "play third base for the Chicago Cubs" in answer to question 2. As you can see, I'm not much for planning and goal setting. Why not, you ask? It's just that I've simplified my life to the point where it no longer makes sense to worry about making or not making goals that I used to set to please everyone but me.

This business places a great deal of emotional strain on a good producer. You have plenty to do and not enough time to do it. If you keep a pocket planner for your appointments, what else do you need?

Your commission statement gives you your policyholder information which you can plug into your pocket planner. Since you don't attend company conventions, sales meetings, and the like, you don't have to worry about them. If you want to take a vacation, just take it when you can. Or, mark down a time for a vacation and when that time comes, just go.

The yearly MDRT meeting is MANDATORY and since it's usually held at the end of June you can pretty well plug that in.

What about plotting your progress?

You made sales or you didn't. The commission statement tells you how well you're doing and how well you've done (renewals). If you get some money each month you're meeting your goal: to make money. What you do today, projected out, shows you exactly what will be happening down the road.

You also know what's going to happen to the industry this year. There will be no strikes, no shortage of product, no need for capital investment, no accounts receivable financing, and if there's a recession in your existing market you can simply move over to another market.

You really don't need to waste your time on planning other than to follow a simple formula like Ben Feldman's "three applications a week" plan. Or, make three calls every day or whatever. Just plan what you're going to do today. Take it one day at a time ... because that's all you really have. What you do day after day will produce your success ... the future is made up of today.

Isn't that nice? Don't you feel better?

The Competition

There isn't any.

Don't let general agents, unit managers, or home office people con you into thinking you need to "know the competition" and that the company's latest gimmick is important.

Most of the agents in America are busy attending meetings and pushing blue, yellow, green, and white cards from one side of a gray box to the other and "supervising" their secretaries. Very few are out in the street selling life insurance.

If you happen to run into a situation where another agent is making a pitch, just back off. I don't care how good a case appears to be, save time, heartache, and money. Compliment the customer on having an agent and build up the company the agent represents. Ask the customer to call if he needs a second opinion, but assure him that he's in good hands.

Drop a note to the agent you just complimented explaining what you've done. Build a good clean reputation in your area ... and guess what will happen. That agent will love you. You'll wear a big white hat in his book ... and he'll be your biggest booster.

Oh, I can hear your cries of anguish. "But what about our super-duper dividend in the 18th year?" Or: "What about the fact that even if the guy gets fungus of the mungus we cover him completely?"

Look, turkey, if you work for a quality company, they're going to pay claims. The main problem is that THERE AREN'T GOING TO BE MANY CLAIMS TO PAY IF YOU SIT IN MEETINGS AND HOME OFFICE CONVENTIONS INSTEAD OF TAKING YOUR PRODUCT TO THE STREET AND SELLING IT!

What good is a dividend on a policy that never gets sold? You could take the worst life product with the highest net cost and still do a great service by putting it in force on someone who is very definitely going to die and who might become disabled.

If all the energy, money, and time spent by companies, general agents, managers, and agents in mental masturbation about products intended to "beat the socks off the competition" ... if all that energy were spent getting in front of people, we could knock sales off the map.

Pick up a hammer and nails ... put down that sledge hammer. Be a builder ... not a destroyer.

The only competition you have is ... YOU!

Commissisons

Put down this book. Go get the MDRT directory. (It's mailed to members each year and lists the names and addresses of all the members.) In the front of the directory you'll find a listing of companies and how many MDRT members each one has. Now go get the big *Best's* book put out each year by the Best's Company. It lists the companies, the financial situation of each, a breakdown of their investment income, and so on. The first paragraph on each company usually mentions approximately how many agents are under contract.

Divide the number of agents by the number of MDRT members. You'll soon see that the top 10 or 15 mutual companies have the highest percentage of MDRT members. Find your company. How does it compare? Find the company you're thinking about joining because it pays such high commissions and promises so much help with your career. Isn't it strange how companies that talk the most about commissions seem to have only 2 or 3 MDRT members?

New York Life pays 55% on permanent and 35% on term and has a strange way of handling renewals (at least I think it's strange) but they have more MDRT members than anyone! Northwestern Mutual has the reputation (among my friends anyway) of being the cheapest and stingiest company on compensation in the business and they are second in MDRT memberships!

The point is this : If commissions are so important, how come these two companies have over 2,000 MDRT members? How come? It's simple: What's 120% of nothing? Nothing.

Take a real hard look at some of those high commission products. Would you buy them? Would you buy permanent, cash value life insurance from that company? Why not? Then how can you possibly think you can sell, day after day, large volumes of their insurance just because you're getting a high commission?

Sure, you might do well for a few months, maybe a few years ... while the blood dripping down your mouth is still fresh. But after a steady diet of your customers' blood, you're going to start to stink, and when you stink no one will want to get near you ... at least not very often. And then too, you do look in the mirror once in a while, don't you?

Don't make the mistake of thinking commissions make you successful. Even if you only got the standard New York commission with no production bonus commission, if you sold policies week after week, you'd be a wealthy person ... and you'd be your own person.

Renewals

Renewal commissions ... oh how you are sold on them when you come into this business!

Remember the guy recruiting you showing the charts of the "average" agent in the company and how all that money flowed in year after year? Wow! Just think, you can work for about five or ten years and have an income for life!

Look: you are never going to get your renewals. Some way, some how, you're going to be screwed out of them. Read your contract. It probably states that you can be terminated with or without cause upon 30 days written notice. Now go to your vesting schedule. You're not 100% vested for maybe 14 years or more ... and in some companies you're never vested!

Look at the hammer over your head! Get a block of premium in force and start looking around at other companies or placing business elsewhere or start shooting off your mouth about the stupid policies of the home office or the general agent .....

Once you've been in this business for a few years they "gotcha!"

So, I suggest that you ignore renewals and keep your freedom. If you get them, fine ... but don't count on them. Don't figure them into any budget. Don't get any fixed expenses based on renewal income, even if you're not a rebel or placing business outside your company. Live on first year commissions.

Your renewals are your profits. Treat them as such, just like a company treats its net profits. Invest your renewals or put them in the bank or into cash value life insurance. BUT DON'T EVER ... EVER ... EVER COUNT ON THEM OR BECOME A SLAVE TO THEM!

Remember, the greatest gift this business gives you is true independence. Keep it by not being fooled by renewals you may never see.

CLU

For many, many years a bunch of hardworking people have tried to put together a program that would not only help you learn the finer points of this business but would also upgrade how the public in general and professionals in particular think about our business.

Out came the Chartered Life Underwriter program. (I've always wondered why they didn't use the word "certified" like CPAs do. I've never liked the word "chartered" but I guess there must be some reason behind it. There always is.)

Anyway, this program seems to be real good. I've never taken any of the courses because I just don't know enough about people yet and haven't read the MDRT proceedings from last year completely through. And I haven't set up any type of regular time to study because I'm not a regular type of guy.

Besides, I really don't care to read about how social security works or what it does because I don't sell social security.

I don't care to know how life insurance premiums are calculated or how the reserve system works. I'm afraid that if I knew all that I might start telling someone.

But you see, this business has something for everyone. There are folks who really get their kicks knowing this stuff, and good for them! I just resent it when people start telling us that we should take CLU because we "need" it or "should" have it or such.

The only fault I find with CLU -- and this isn't the Institute's doing -- is that far too many weak managers tell agents that CLU will make them great agents, that they'll be respected as professionals. The implication is that once you're a professional, you don't have to get out and sell any more .....

And then there's that word ... *professional*. We are salespeople, we get paid commissions. Professionals charge fees. We hire professionals to work for us. Salespeople make $400, $1,000 or more per hour. Few professionals charge over $80, so who wants to be a professional?

I wonder why I'm supposed to know all about estate planning and how to calculate estate taxes when there are top-notch attorneys who can do it for me, leaving me more time to build relationships.

I'm not much for all this estate planning, not really. My own will and trust are not up to par any more, but I do have a

---

million of life insurance on me. You can do a lot with a million, and that's what I tell many of my customers: "If you don't want to go through all that estate planning stuff just buy a couple of million, give it to your spouse, and forget the rest. Your babies will be safe and your spouse can have good times with a million."

I guess that's too easy. A CLU would go in with thirty pages of nonsense, screw around for six months, and the customer would get cancer or die in the meantime. At least, that's my impression .....

Consider: There's an underwriter's association in Southern California with about 154 CLUs and only 13 MDRT. Sure are a lot of starving professionals out there in insurance land .....

I guess I've turned off a lot of serious, talented, and successful agents with that remark, but that's how the situation looks to me. I remember too many folks in my first agency who were studying CLU and starving. The ones who made it all have their big plaques on the wall and they seem real proud of their accomplishment. I'd like to have one of those plaques and the initials after my name too, if I didn't have to work for it or study .....

Not that it would get me a sale or increase my social prestige because eventually we have to get out there and make sales to put life insurance in force. Sooner or later we have to call on someone face to face, with or without the initials after our names.

My recommendation is this: Until you get MDRT, don't start CLU. First read *Tax Facts*, Mass Mutual's great book *Business Continuation Agreements*, and the last three years of MDRT proceedings. Also listen to the MDRT meeting tapes for the last three years and to Ray Tripplet's tape "The Dramatics and Semantics of a Sale." THEN start CLU.

Here's another thought: Study only when you're paid to study. I'm a real tiger on closely held corporations. Why? Because as I got into the business, I'd discover a problem, go look it up and learn the solution or listen in as an attorney gave the answer at a meeting I initiated with the customer and his attorney.

On the other hand, I've never done much with partnerships, so I don't know a thing about them and couldn't care less. If I get involved with a partnership one day, THEN I'll hit the books. Study only when you're being paid.

Here's a short-form CLU course:

If people in business don't have business continuation agreements, they should.

If they don't have wills, they should, and maybe trusts.

If they're rich, they have estate taxes to pay on themselves and their spouses. They can use their money or life insurance. Sometimes ours is cheaper.

If they have a "key man," they should consider insuring that person.

If they have children, the kids probably should have some insurance for when they are older.

If they are covered by social security, they shouldn't count on it to protect their families.

If they don't understand life insurance, tell them you don't either. When they turn on the radio they don't know how IT works ... they just turn on the switch and it works because the manufacturer DOES know how radios work. Tell them that your manufacturer, Mutual Life of USA (or whatever), has been around for over a hundred years. They pay the premium and when they die their spouses get the money. It's just like the radio: they buy it and it works.

If they want to know how life insurance premiums are calculated, tell them you don't know but that you'll get them a book from CLU and they can read it.

Guess that does it for CLU. It's great to go for and you'll learn good stuff ... after you've learned to sell and can afford the time and distraction. I think I'll go after mine when I retire. I WOULD like to know how all those numbers in the rate book go together .....

Secretaries

One of the major causes of agent failure or mediocrity is call reluctance. Picking up the phone or going out the door invites rejection. So you don't do either, at least not as much as "they" say you should.

One way to overcome call reluctance is to NOT have a secretary.

When a call comes in, you have to answer it. If you're not there, you have to return the call. There's nobody there to say, "Is there something I can help you with?"

Think for a moment. If the secretary takes care of the problem without having to "bother" you, you've missed a great opportunity to talk with a customer and maybe try for an appointment or share an exciting idea you "just heard."

When a customer calls to check on cash values, it's for a reason. There's a problem. It's a call made TO you, not FROM you. You didn't pick up the phone and risk rejection, the CUSTOMER did. It's your opportunity to find out what's wrong, to see if you can help .....

What about all the paperwork? Don't create paperwork. Don't file things. What kinds of files do you need? The general agent and the home office have records of everything, including the last time your customer belched. If you need to know something, just ask the agency manager or the home office. They'll leap to your help ... they're there just waiting for your call.

Carry beneficiary change and ownership change forms in a box in your car. Keep some at home and in your office. Keep envelopes right next to them along with some stamps. When the call comes in fill out the form, stick a stamp on it, and TALK to the customer. It's another time for presenting a sales idea, sharing a mutual problem, talking about a baseball team's chances ... it's another customer contact, YOU BIG DUMMY! Without rejection!!!

Birthday cards? Age changes? Why not have a big desk calendar and ONCE A YEAR spend a few hours listing all the folks on it? Have the cards in a pile in your desk ... the stamps are right there ... YOU write a note on the card ... YOU put on the smiley face ... YOU get the feeling of really caring, of making the customer happy by remembering. Don't be a phoney and have some clerk send a card you don't even know about .....

Another good point about not having a secretary is that you need to be busy. You need to "feel" like you're working in the old fashioned sense. When you knock out a pile of paperwork, you feel good, and you really know what's going on in your business. (And don't be afraid to learn how to type by buying a book at the bookstore.)

Making appointments for you? Baloney!!! YOU make appointments so you know what the hell you're doing. YOU make those calls. YOU are the only one who can smell a sale or a chance for one. Getting appointments for interviews on a favorable basis so that you can demonstrate the value of your product is the most critical aspect of the business ... and you want to delegate it to some snot-nosed kid who's probably thinking about her boyfriend?

Opening your mail? Just throw the stuff away. You're under no obligation to read every piece of junk someone sends you, especially local brokers. You know what the home office is going to send you. Just pick up your mail and say "THIS IS MY ENEMY!" and start throwing it out immediately! The only mail you look at is mail from a customer and the commissision statement from your company. The rest is garbage and only gives you an excuse to avoid being productive.

Until you're earning well over $100,000 per year in first year commissions, there's no reason to have a secretary. Anyone who says you should ... well ... make sure that that person pays the salary.

Many general agents are now beginning to go along with the above comments and have formed "pools" of secretaries who will type a letter or perform other chores for you without becoming a part of your operation.

I suppose you could use a secretary AFTER you become successful so that you could get more fun out of the business by delegating some of the more routine tasks ... BUT NOT UNTIL THEN! Build your business from profits. When you have money in the bank and are really cranking in the business, then take a hard look ... but not until then.

Paperwork -- Why Agents Think They Hate It

So many good agents are torn apart inside because of an constant struggle to give good service, to take a personal interest in "details," to be "organized," to be effective and efficient.

You hate your desk because it's a mess. You're afraid to take time off because you'll lose momentum. You fight paperwork. In short, you're in a continual state of frustration and think you must hire a big staff and so on .....

Here's what's wrong. Here's what you don't know about this business. From this point on you're not going to be frustrated because you're going to UNDERSTAND THE PROBLEM.

When you make a sale you are mentally in 18th gear going down the highway in an 18-wheeler. The pen touches the paper ... you have a sale! It took high-level, high-gear thought power to build the relationship, state the problem, demonstrate how your product removes obstacles to the customer's objectives ... to support the customers during the "is this the right thing to do?" time, to reinforce their ability to make a good decision. You expanded their thinking, you helped them grow.

You get in the car, drive back to the office, and fill out the rest of the application. You downshift to 4th gear ... you JOLT your brain. The phone rings and a beneficiary change problem comes through or a request for a cash value update or a new requirement for underwriting on a case you submitted two weeks ago. You downshift to 3rd gear.

You leave for a week ... you lose momentum ... and when you come back, you have to go through mail from brokers, home office baloney, agency information. You're in 1st gear and grinding. You have an appointment to make a sales call and you're expected to shift from 1st, 3rd, all the way up to 18th on the drive to see the customer .....

You're an emotional yo-yo! There's nothing wrong with your ability to handle detail. You can handle detail as well as anyone ... if that's what your job is for a period of time. You're a good money manager and you're a good customer service follow-through person ... if that's what you're doing for a period of time.

But you just can't jump from one to the other, just as a big rig can't jump from 18th to 4th and back without breaking down and throwing the load all over the road.

So don't be so hard on yourself. Understand the problem. YOU make YOUR own rules. Why not set Saturday morning or maybe all day Friday aside for ALL detail, check writing, service work, cash value requests, and so on. During the rest of the week roll down the road in 18th gear. Don't let anyone downshift your rig. NOTHING can't wait another day or three or four. If you get a service request, tell the customer it'll be done on Friday (or whatever day you pick).

Remember: You get the most miles per gallon in high gear.

Your Title -- Or, What You Do For a Living

What's on your business card? Your stationery?

What do you tell people you do for a living when they meet you for the first time?

Well, there is no right title or wrong title. There's just the title you feel most comfortable with ... but I mean really comfortable. You don't want to be a phoney. So, you aren't an estate planner, financial consultant, or such. You sell life insurance and maybe some related products like group or disability.

That's how you get paid. That's what you do for a living. And here lies one of the most negative aspects of this business ... little or no social prestige. The minute you tell the average Joe that you sell life insurance, you're pretty much put in a slot in the guy's brain, unless he's a rare bird who has the services of a top agent.

I still want to throw up when I tell someone that I sell life insurance for a living. I've tried all sorts of things like saying, "I sell money." Oh, you're a banker? "No, bankers lend you money ... I sell it" and so on ... even producing dollar bills and selling the guy "samples" for two or three pennies each and making him keep them because I'm proud of my samples .... then if he wants more tell him I'll stop by his office and explain my great business to him .....

That works ... anything you do works ... if you just do it .....

Another idea that I used for a while was to say I was a life insurance "buyer." What do you mean? I'd say that there are about 1,800 life insurance companies and each one has about 30 products. That's about 54,000 choices, so I help people buy the right plan for them.

Trouble was, I only sold for one company so that was a lot of baloney. But it worked, so I used it. Anything you do works ... if you just do it .....

Here's another one: "I figure out how long people are going to live." That's a real grabber, especially when you pull this on an old codger. How do you do that? "I do an estimate of your life expectancy and when I get the answer I tell you how long you're going to live so you can figure out what to do and when." How do you do that? "I send you to one of my estimators. Would you like to know how long you're going to live?"

That one is a lot of fun and it works. Anything you do works ... if you just do it .....

Right now I have "Kent P. Larsen, Inc." on my card with the slogan "Bringing People and Ideas Together" below it. I guess it's okay for now ... I'll use it, but I'll probably do something else when the supplies run out. That's the great thing about this business. You run your own show. You can do anything you want, whatever fits.

******

To be honest, I guess this whole question still bothers me. What I'd really like to say when someone asks what I do for a living is: "I sell life insurance, you ignorant jerk, and if you say one word I'll punch your lights out!"

I guess I still have an identity problem .....

Your Car and the Way You Dress

You worry about this? If so, it shows how screwed up you are. I say this from experience. I've blown more money on cars than most agents make in a year or two or three. I kept trying to drive the "right" one, to project an "image," to look successful so people would listen to me. I've had a Mercedes 4.5 SE, a Seville, a Sedan Deville ... you name it.

At this point, I AM successful and people don't listen to me any more than they did before. When I realized this fact, I went out and got the car I wanted, a VW Rabbit Diesel. (I love it!)

I've tried wearing conservative suits, sport jackets, no jackets, sweatshirts, slacks and white short-sleeved shirts with a tie and without, rings ... even put on one of those gold chains once and opened my shirt to show the hairs .....

I finally figured out that when I made calls I sold insurance and that when I didn't make calls I didn't sell insurance. People treated me nice when I was nice and they treated me nasty when I was nasty.

It doesn't make a bit of difference what you wear as long as you're comfortable. Make a call on a banker in a tee-shirt and sandals and you probably won't be comfortable.

Dress however and drive whatever makes you happy and comfortable. When you're relaxed, confident, and happy you make others feel the same way. You don't have to drive a big expensive car to make people like and respect you. Your warm smile and sincere approach -- that's the ticket!

If you're still confused and don't know what to do, here's a rule I learned from an oldtime salesman: "Drive the car your customers drive, wear the clothes your customers wear."

One point for you folks wanting to tune up your percentage and be more effective: Study the impact of color as a communication vehicle. Study the effect of wearing a brown suit vs. a blue suit. Learn what combinations have been scientifically tested to give the first impression that you're a person to be trusted. It's great stuff and there are some great books on it ... see the "Recommended Reading" list later in this book.

But remember, if you don't make calls you won't have these problems. You won't have a car to drive or clothes to wear.

Your Office

As soon as you can, get out of the general agency. Get an office by yourself or with another agent. As soon as you do you're on your way to really learning what this business is all about. Until you take this step you take the terrible chance of being influenced and distracted by all the baloney going on around you.

Once you move out of the agency, customers will come to your office from time to time. If it happens only a few times a month it'll more than pay for the office.

Don't get an office in the same building as the general agency. That's still too close. Agents will stop by and distract you. It'll be too easy for you to run upstairs to chit chat, bother other agents, or get into trouble shooting your mouth off.

And don't work out of your home unless you absolutely have to. If your spouse is at home also, you run the risk of becoming a "honey do." Your spouse says sweetly "Honey, can you do this ..." or "Honey, can you do that ..." Spouses need their privacy. You need yours. Having an office or a corner at home for doing work is fine but it just can't be the whole enchillada.

Sometimes you need to get away from people, from everyone. You need to be able to go into your own little hole and hide occasionally. Having an office filled with things you put there comforts you when you've been kicked in the teeth by business or your family. It keeps you from getting into trouble.

Get an office as close to your home as possible. This way, when you get an idea you can run down there in just a few minutes. And maybe your kids can stop after school and visit you. Let them clean up the furniture for a buck and watch you work. They won't stay long ... and it's fantastic!

Your office doesn't need to be downtown or in the financial district. Customers aren't going to come and see you on a regular basis unless you want to specialize in selling to high-roller professionals in the financial market ... and play in their league. Some people can pull this off ... you and I probably can't. We want our customers to be comfortable with us. They're probably more comfortable in their own place or in a tavern over a couple of beers.

And you and I don't buy this stuff about trying to get the customers "on our own turf" like we're going to take advantage of them or something. You don't have to worry about your chair

---

being higher than theirs ... sometimes I sit on the floor or kneel down at the desk while working on something. That other stuff is for the movies and people who want their egos stroked more than they want a sale.

You don't need a reception area, either. When customers open the door to my office, they're in it. If someone else is there I introduce them and we shoot the breeze. Low key, no formality, no big deal. We're all friends and pals. You need insurance, everybody needs insurance. You like me and I like you, so you buy the stuff from me and then we can talk about the important things in life.

Don't furnish your office with the idea that you've got to impress the world. Furnish it the way you feel comfortable. If possible, try to establish a theme such as sailing or sports in general, a fun theme that expresses your individual personality and makes you a little different.

Get a good typewriter, an electric one so that things you type look good. Don't skimp -- get the best. Get good calculators and have them everywhere.

Get a portable computer terminal (I got mine from Texas Instruments for under $2,000) and call Agency Computer Systems (ACS) in Encino, California. In my opinion, theirs is the best life insurance information service, designed by folks who actually sell life insurance. Their instruction book will teach you more about life insurance and how it works than any other single source. They also have all the major companies on computer so you can run a ledger statement on just about anyone if your customer wants to know about other companies or if you're interested in other products just for your own information.

How any of you can be without this service is beyond me. You depend on home office proposals which are designed, for the most part, by folks who don't know how to sell but sure can fill up a page with numbers .....

Taking this machine and putting it down in front of a CPA or a tax attorney is more fun than just about anything. They don't believe a word you say but when that machine starts cranking out the numbers on estate taxes, inflation, or a ledger showing a cost comparison between term and whole life, they go nuts! And they usually ask me to run a program on them.

I don't use mine more than once or twice a year, but remember I have steady customers now and a lot of skills that eliminate some of the need for it. But it's always in my car and ready to go ... a valuable item for any insurance salesman's tool box.

Understanding Your Co-Workers

No matter what business you're in, there are people other than customers with whom you must work.

Salespeople, high-energy ones especially, seem to demand perfect performance from themselves. You beat yourself to death doing your BEST. So, what happens to your relationships with your co-workers? You usually expect them to be perfect, find fault, and beat the hell out of them. After all, you're out on the front lines selling while they're back in their comfortable, risk-less environments. They should jump with appreciation at your every request, right?

Even if they're quite competent, we salespeople just have to find fault somewhere and then attack them and gossip or complain about them. We get away with it most of the time, too.

Why do we do it?

For the same reason we kick the dog and yell at the kids after a hard day's work ... because we can get away with it.

If we talked to a customer that way, we wouldn't get the sale. Pain and punishment, immediate and certain.

But the family? They're stuck with us. Managers, home office people? They're stuck with us to a lesser degree so we give them SLIGHTLY better treatment and consideration.

There's another problem, however. These people, by nature, are DIFFERENT from us ... and this difference is what we want to explore in this section. We want to understand the difference so we won't expect so much from them.

I think you could sum up relationship problems with management in just two horrible words ... "high expectations." We expect management people to react and respond in much the same way we do to our customers ... and they don't and never will. That's why we're paid so much more than they are when we work our craft and use our skills.

So, let's discuss these people and then let's get on with our work and not bring any of this up ever again .....

General Agents

General agents come in all shapes and sizes. Many of them are "great salespeople" in that after failing in the life insurance business, they somehow sold the home office on the idea of making them general agents or managers.

Sure, there are exceptions. There are former top agents who wanted to try management because they thought it an even greater challenge ... but oh, how rare they are and how few of them make it. Most wind up back in personal production after a few years of wetnursing young agents and fighting the home office.

The general agent is the focal point of an agent's discontent. Agents blame the general agent for every failure and take credit for every accomplishment ... because they don't understand just what general agents can and cannot do, just what general agents should and should not do .....

Your general agent CANNOT go out and make calls for you .....

Your general agent CANNOT get you to sit on the pot at 3 a.m. and read *Tax Facts* or MDRT proceedings .....

Your general agent CANNOT be with you day and night watching how you spend YOUR money .....

Give the folks a break. After they recruit you and teach you the basics, get off their backs. Stop trying to make them into something they're not. How can they teach you multimillion dollar production techniques if they never had them? How can they get into your skin and know what method is best for you?

At best your general agent is a batting coach. Imagine Pete Rose asking HIS batting coach at Cincinnatti, Ted Klususki, to take a look at his swing. Ted tells Pete to move his right foot forward half an inch and Pete's average goes up two points that season. BUT: Ted didn't give Pete what it takes to be a star. Pete got that himself, when he was in high school, in the winters alone in a gym, on the field with heart and guts. All Ted did was re-check the basics for Pete ... and that's all your general agent can ever do for you.

Does your general agent look a bit different in that light?

Now that you know what general agents do, stay away from them unless you need help getting a rated case issued standard, an advance from the home office, or help with your divorce.

A Note to General Agents

You general agents reading this book -- let me ask you a few questions .....

Instead of telling agents to "get more activity," why don't you go out and get some activity of your own?

How many CPAs, lawyers, trust officers, and bankers did you call this week to tell them about your agency, your company, and the professional approach your group is taking in its attempt to solve financial problems?

How many gifts of *Tax Facts* or the latest advanced underwriting material did you send to these people? How many phone calls did you make to follow up your "gift" and tell your agency's story?

How many seminars did you put on this year for local professionals ... in lieu of quarterly contest "outings" that cost a ton of money and accomplish absolutely nothing?

How many fishing trips did you arrange for top members of the financial community with a couple "stars" as hosts ... instead of sending 30 young agents back to a home office convention?

How much needless paperwork did you take from agents this week? How many times did you walk the halls and tell agents to get out of the office?

How many of your agents' personal programs did you check to see if they're up to date and adequate? Do all your agents have wills? Business continuation agreements? Coverage on their spouses, on their children? Disability? Do they have letters to their clients recommending another agent if they die tonight?

Shoes for the cobbler's children. YOU be their agent. YOU sell them insurance and financial planning ... personally. You may not make the Round Table but you'll sure have a successful agency. If agents can't buy this business for themselves and their families, they can't sell it, can they?

(By the way: how's YOUR program, Ms. or Mr. General Agent?)

Home Office Officials

Home office officials mean well .....

They try real hard ... but with rare exception, nature and life didn't give them the equipment they need to be of real help to you. Check your home office people out. How many ever sold a policy? How many were ever truly successful selling the product?

How can they possibly relate to you? They are corporate people living in a different world. They're like farmers tilling the soil and going home each night. You ... you're a hunter. When you kill you eat. When you don't kill you don't eat. You can't be put into a corporate cage or do the things corporate people seem so able and so willing to do: plan ... administer ... keep records. You are creative, people oriented, and full of life, a free spirit with unlimited horizons. You left the corporate womb to find your own place in the sun. You wanted a dream, not a promise or a guarantee.

Be nice to the people in your home office ... but stay away from them. They are MAJOR distractions. They are a MAJOR obstacle in your way to a successful selling career. They can pull you, push you, torment you with their endless streams of ribbons, awards, and games. They can stuff your mind with endless reams of paper filled with logic, when you sell to EMOTIONS. They can dazzle you with their latest dippy-do product or new 18-column ledger statement.

Stop reading home office stuff until you're in the MDRT. Most of it was written by people who can't sell and never could, or by lawyers who couldn't make it as lawyers, let alone selling. Don't read anything from the home office except your commission statement. Don't get involved in arguments over new commission structures if you're new to the business. You're not selling enough at this point in your career to make a difference, so why waste time over commission schedules and proposed policy changes if you don't have commissions or policies?

Leave home office stuff to home office people. They try to involve you only because they don't know any better. You can't do much for them and they can't do much for you until you're successful. So let's leave all this to our fellow agents who've been in the business for 20 years ... they have the time and the big renewal accounts to handle it.

What you need is a sale and you can't sell anything to the home office!

A Note to Home Office People

To you home office people: If you're wondering what you can do to help agents aside from leaving them alone, here are some thoughts for you .....

Have you ever really looked at the type of advertising your company does, your TV commercials, magazine ads, and industry publication ads? They prove, at least to me, that you really don't place much value on the agent in the scheme of things .....

Prudential: You want people to buy a "piece of the rock." New York Life: I think you're selling football or footballs. Every time I watch one of these commercials I feel sick inside. They may be smart advertising schemes, but they certainly don't help agents feel good about themselves .....

State Farm is about the only company I've seen that really demonstates its care and concern for agents and how it values its agency force. Take a look at how the agent is highlighted in all their ads. Here in California, especially Southern California, State Farm has a WAITING LIST made up mostly of agents already in the business working for other companies! They also require that a prospective agent show that he or she has at least $15,000 in reserve before joining them. It's also my understanding that the average State Farm agent in Southern California earns around $78,000 a year!

You home office officials have had over 100 years to get your act together but you haven't done it ... because you don't understand your own business. You don't know how to train agents, you don't know how to treat them, and you don't know how to sell them to the public.

Too harsh? Too tough? Too broad a statement? You have convicted yourselves by the very fact that only three or four agents out of a hundred make the Million Dollar Round Table ... that most have poverty level incomes ... that your own agents for the most part don't have even minimum personal programs.

No use beating you folks to death. As I said in the beginning of this piece, you mean well ... you try hard. Take a look at the type of advertising you should be doing, the type that will help the agent .....

Imagine it's Sunday evening. The American people are watching "60 Minutes." It's commercial time ......

A guy dressed in a nice suit and tie appears on the screen walking down a city street. The camera comes in close and he says .....

"Hi! My name's Joe. I'm a life insurance salesman. You don't want to see me today. I called, but you were busy. You see, you didn't want to talk to me. You don't know much about life insurance except that it takes money to buy it, and you don't know much about me or if you can trust me to tell you the truth. And how many salesmen in your life have told you the truth?"

(He walks up to a business door.)

"You won't see me ... but somehow I convinced Sam, the owner of this business, to see me. In a few minutes I'm going to give Sam some ideas on how to increase his profits, save taxes, keep his people from leaving, how to buy out his partner with before-tax dollars ... oh, countless ideas.

"Sam's attorney didn't call him today with these ideas. His CPA didn't either. In fact, when Sam gets excited about these ideas, the first thing he'll do is call one of these guys. And then I'll go over and see them. Eventually, the ideas will be put to work. Sam will be happy and I might get him to buy a life insurance policy."

(He opens the door and turns.)

"Oh, and don't let me forget to tell you. This evening I'm delivering a check to a widow, a woman who was married to a guy like Sam for 30 years, watching him kill himself building his business. I'm going there tonight to give her a check ... a big check ... a tax-free check. This morning she went to see the attorney and the CPA her husband employed. They gave her bills. I'm the only one giving her a check.

"And you folks don't want to see me. I wonder why."

******

What company has the guts? NONE. We should all chip in and put a couple hundred thousand together and put this TV ad on ourselves. If YOU want to start this thing going, send me a letter and I'll mail you a check.

Underwriters

Underwriters are not the enemy. If you are fortunate enough to work with a company that allows you direct contact with underwriters you'll soon find that they are a very special breed of cat .....

All they want out of life is to be able to trust you. If you just don't sandbag them, if you tell them the truth and build a good reputation with them, well, when a "gray" area comes along, when a case could go either way, they'll help you, not hurt you.

A cover letter on any case involving something special helps. Remember, all they see is the paper in front of them. They don't see the emotion. They don't hear the guy pump his heart out. They don't see how much you love and respect him. They haven't watched him lose his stomach and his family building his business. They don't see you bleed for the guy when he tells you how tired he is of hitting the ball day after day and getting kicked in the head .....

Share it with them.

Be open. Let them participate in the great value you help generate through life insurance policies that tell people they're worth something ... even if deep down they're having a hard time believing it themselves .....

Underwriters in the home office ... friends, not foes, if you treat them with the same respect that want to show you .....

Technicians and Specialists

Far too often, a weak manager brings in a "specialist" he's trying to promote to you, someone who isn't a salesperson but rather a technician (who probably owes the manager or general agent money). This technical person pulls you down, gets you off course, and scares the hell out of you with how much you don't know about A-B Trusts and the correct procedure for estate tax planning and the like .....

Remember, technical things don't mean much unless you have sales to be technical about. Until you're selling, don't get too concerned with technical matters. You might try to tell your customers about your knowledge and confuse them to the point that they lose sight of a simple fact: that they might die someday and someone who loves them might suffer.

Look ... here are all the products you need .....

Whole life:

1. Level premium with full use of dividends.

2. Graded premium with at least three years of reduced premium. (A ten-year increasing product is best.)

3. A combination of permanent and term with the dividend frozen into trading in the term automatically each year. This premium is in between the level and graded product.

Term:

1. Annual and renewable term until age 70 or 100 with waiver of premium that will allow conversion to whole life and pay the whole life premium.

2. The contractual right to go back with an original age conversion for at least three years. A few good companies allow you to pay for ten years and then make an original age conversion.

I'll go into how you use these tools later. The point here is that if you have these products you don't need to look at anything else the technicians want to show you.

Brokerage Managers

Just as soon as it looks like you have a beachhead established in the business and make MDRT you'll start receiving all kinds of the wrong type of attention .....

First will come direct mail from other companies soliciting your "surplus business," the business your company doesn't want. That's a lie. They want ALL of your business. The term "surplus business" is an opiate used to gloss over the theft of your time and talent from the company that took you through the toughest stages of your career.

Throw all this junk out. You won't learn a thing ... absolutely nothing. Don't even open the mail you receive. Don't waste your time. When you go to the MDRT meeting you can talk to the folks you meet from other companies and find out if there's anything really sharp that you should know about. You'll be telling them about your stuff too. Once a year is about all the time you should take .....

Next you'll have brokerage managers calling on the phone, wanting to show you what their whippy-do companies have to offer you. Let's say you agree to meet with one of these guys .....

In almost all cases, the commission will be higher than you're getting now and that's the first thing he'll show you. Next he'll give you case after case (no names, just Betty B. and John D.) of other companies issuing rated policies and his company issuing standard just two days after he got the medical and application.

This whole meeting will be very warm and he'll listen to ANYTHING you want to tell him. He'll sympathize with you, nod his head wisely when you complain about your general agent, and then, with a knowing smile, look skyward in almost prayer-like form and say, "You're well known in the area and have a flawless reputation as a true professional even though you've only been in the business a little over two years. I'll keep my ears open and get back to you. Our regional manager is coming out toward the end of the week ... everything in confidence, I assure you ... maybe there's something we can do for you ....."

Believe me, you'll get a call from his regional manager, either that afternoon or first thing the next day. It'll be a mystery call. No name ... just like in the movies ... and you'll be very impressed. After all, here you are knocking yourself out for the chance to present your product to customers who don't want to see you, and now YOU are the one someone wants to see.

A meeting is arranged ... stroke, stroke ... boy, they make you feel good! They leave you a copy of their agent contract. You take it home and read it ... twice the commission if you do two times the business you're currently producing! You tell yourself you can double your production because these people UNDERSTAND you .....

YOU DUMB JERK! If you leave your agency now, you deserve your fate. If you read my piece on general agents and what they can and can't do for you, you understand that changing companies isn't going to help you, dummy! In fact, it'll reduce your credibility with your current customers. Remember how you told them they were buying the world's greatest insurance value .....?

There are legitimate brokerage managers who really do just want the business your company can't write. If you're approached by a brokerage manager and can't decide if he's on the level or not, test him. Offer him a standard issue case and see if he'll turn it down. See if he'll call your general agent and say that he just can't in good conscience take advantage of your inexperience. See if he'll ask the general agent to talk with you about the policy, saying that you should be placing it with your company and not his.

Dream on! He's out for himself and doesn't care about your career or your customers. He's wasting your valuable time and the only thing he's accomplishing is to puff up your ego. Isn't it nice to have someone calling on YOU, trying to sell YOU insurance? Grow up!

Save time and heartache and don't even talk to these people. You won't leave anyhow. Your general agent will talk you out of it ... or maybe you owe him money.

You do need a very special type of relationship with a very special type of brokerage manager. Find out just who that person is by calling the life and qualifying members of the MDRT in your area. Ask them who does a truly professional job with quality products in the area of high risk substandard business.

One name will start to pop up. Call that person and solve this terrible problem. Work with him. Don't cheat on him. Give him all your business that cannot be placed realistically with your company. Be loyal to him and you'll give your customers the benefit of his great service. Remember, the sick person REALLY needs our product.

In a nutshell, stay away from ALL brokerage managers except the one you've picked out to serve your sick ones .....

Lawyers and Accountants

Before you say you hate lawyers and accountants, think for a minute about what they do for a living.

Accountants are historians. They record things that already happened. Why businessmen place them in the position of making decisions is the wonder of the ages.

A lawyer is trained to tear things apart and find reasons why they won't work. They're the ones, not you, who sign their names to a document protecting your customer against errors and omissions. They're the ones who have to defend your customer in court or before the IRS, not you.

The fact that so many lawyers and accountants set themselves up as God's gift to the world is the result of people in business not knowing anyone else to turn to and not having the time to take away from their businesses to study these fields or research their own problems.

The lawyer and the accountant are placed in terrible positions by us. We threaten the daylights out of them. They've learned that the easiest way to handle us is simply not to see us, to put us down, treat us like dirt, and not return our phone calls. They also know that we make a very good commission if they agree with our proposal ... while they make a fee of $60 or $100 and take the responsibility for the decision off the customer. Why should they put themselves out on a limb?

Lawyers and accountants do not hate life insurance, they do not hate whole life. They just don't know very much about our product. Few have ever had a ledger on $100,000 of whole life properly demonstrated showing flexibility, paid up values, options, waiver of premium as a mini-disability policy, and so on. They won't admit that they can't seem to save much money and probably should have a forced cash accumulation fund so they could take advantage of the investment opportunities they see every day. They don't know what the cost of a million of term is. They probably have association life, health, and disability but no will or trust and no guardian for their children. In other words, they've probably never had the services of a top agent like you.

Oh, and don't forget ... lawyers and accountants don't bill good customers for every request, so they also have to decide if they're going to be paid for greeting you. They sell their time by the hour and costs are going up.

So, if you can, get your customer to agree that when you present an idea to the accountants or attorneys, you can tell them to start the clock. Or, if you have the guts and the imagination, tell the attorneys or accountants that you want to be billed for their time, that you appreciate their value, and that you feel your idea has such merit you're willing to pay for their analysis .....

But nooooooo ... you're probably like most other life insurance agents ... a cheapskate.

This industry has you spoiled rotten. If your home office or general agent won't buy it for you, you don't have it. You simply won't invest in your own business. (And I don't mean a secretary or a fancy office or a big car or an expensive wardrobe.)

Why not have an attorney and a CPA on retainer? You have your guy call your customer's attorney or accountant. They speak the same language and they don't threaten each other. What would this invaluable investment cost? Maybe $2,000 or $3,000 a year, if that, especially if you bring your guy business.

That's how you handle CPAs and attorneys: you buy them, you put them to work for you. You call the shots instead of being the target.

Too simple for you, isn't it? Go ahead ... knock your brains out, get your head kicked in, lose control of your case. Don't listen, cheapskate .....

Big Hitters

Too often agents think that so-called big hitters are somehow different, that they don't sweat, stink, or cry, that they never get into fights or think bad thoughts ... that they're somehow "better" than other people.

This is a myth created by general agents with the cooperation and encouragement of the home office.

In fact, agents who place large amounts of business are USED by management. In most cases management would actually like to get rid of them.

Producers of multimillion dollar annual volumes are the biggest pains the home office has. They rant, rave, fight, demand, and cry ... constantly. And most of them make two, three, four, five, six times the income of ANYONE in the home office, including the president of the company .....

For the most part big producers can't tell you how they sell so much ... and if they try to tell you, you get conflicting stories. Some make a lot of calls, others just a few. Some make 100-page proposals, others use the rate book. Just one thing they seem to have in common ... they know how to get a sale, one way or another, and they do it often enough to make big bucks.

Big producers are just plain folks who come in all sizes, shapes, and styles. They fight with their spouses. They yell at their kids. Some are fat and don't jog five miles a day. Some go to church, some don't. They all get lonely sometimes, just like everyone else.

They are, in almost all cases, the most generous people you'll ever meet, once they know that you accept them for themselves without all the trappings placed on them by management. They're the kind of people we'd all like to have as friends.

Approach big producers as you would anyone else ... as the real person you are, without phoniness.

Remember, the mythical "big hitter" doesn't exist ... there are just little kids with lots of ideas.

Something For the "Old Pros"

I don't mean just age. This is a note to each of you who has really made a success out of yourself in this business. And when I say success I don't mean necessarily big production and a big name. I mean you've reached your goal, you're happy, you make a good living, and you're of value. Maybe you've been in the business 20, 30, or 40 years.

I have some words for you .....

When you go to MDRT make it a point to look for at least five young agents. Pick them out from the agents standing shyly in the background, alone, and looking lonely. They might not be your idea of "sharp comers" either. Maybe they're not even good looking and dress lousy.

Go up and quietly introduce yourself. Ask them to come over and sit down. You just want to know who they are, where they come from, whether they're married or not, if this is the first time they've been here, and so on. Don't tell them how wonderful you are even if they recognize you. Concentrate on asking them how they feel.

Ask for their cards. Tell them you'll write and see how they're doing. Leave them and make some notes on those business cards about their spouses' names, the kids, and such. A few months later drop them a note. You could include a tip on an article they might like to read. Ask them to write you back and tell you how they're doing and if they've used any ideas they picked up at the MDRT meeting.

If you don't do this at MDRT then do it if you go to your company convention. But do it. Year in and year out. You will save careers. You will enrich lives and through these young agents you will sell millions and millions and millions to people who need our product.

At your agency, don't take young agents out for breakfast. Invite them, one at a time, to come over to your home one night during the week for coffee and cake with their spouses and yours. Try not to talk too much about business or ideas. Just be warm. Show them your hobbies. Let them see that they can have security, that the business will work, that life won't always be controlled and uncontrolled panic and frustration. Let their spouses see that maturity will come eventually and that this hell won't last forever.

Do this, folks. It'll fill your heart with love and when you die, lots of agents and their families will come to your bedside and your funeral.

Finding Your Customers

So. You've simplified your life. You've eliminated all those distractions and put all those business relationships in proper perspective. What do you do now? Where do you go in the marketplace? Who do you call on?

The ideas outlined in this section are at odds with the thinking of most of the "teachers" in our business. But that's okay. If our ideas were parallel, I'd be in trouble. (Remember, 90% of the agents selling today are economically poor and only 10% qualify for MDRT membership.)

If you keep doing what most of you are encouraged to do in the marketplace, you have an excellent chance for failure or mediocrity at best.

Here are some solutions to your problems. But: these solutions are valid only if you take ACTION and actually use the information rather than just reading it, being entertained, and "feeling good" for a while. These solutions will work. They'll work because they'll help you focus your efforts for maximum results. They'll give you a comfortable way to sell an uncomfortable product, uncomfortable because it's concerned with death and disability.

Once you've put these solutions to work, don't cast your pearls before swine. There are too few of you. There are too many people who want to see you. Don't waste your time and talents on people who don't feel they need you.

Prospecting

What are you, a coal miner? Do you wear a hard hat with a light on it and carry a gas lantern into the caves?

Do you ride a burro to work or a car? Do you walk around with a metal detector or a rate book?

Oh, how that word rings throughout our industry! Prospecting! The KEY to the business! No wonder so many agents don't want to get out of bed in the morning. The thought of living this day and the rest of your working life looking at people you meet and putting them through a "prospecting funnel" and then onto little colored cards, sending out pre-approach letters with follow-up phone calls and "get-acquainted" interviews, building relationships, educating customers over the years on the value of life insurance in general and of whole life in particular, sending cards or taking customers to lunch on their birthdays, asking for referrals, calling for selling interviews on age changes ... UGH !!!!!!!!

What are you, some kind of mechanical monster? What are the people you meet, entries for your one-card system?

Okay, let's back off a minute and take a look. The above system works ... for a few people. A few agents can stumble along and some even make it big by using approaches based on prospecting and adherance to a "system."

How about you?

Would you like to meet people the way you used to before you got into this business? Remember how nice it was just to say "Hello" and if you liked them, ask what they did? No pressure on you, no pressure on them .....

Would you like your customers to think of you as a friend, someone they can talk to and rely on for help, rather than as a "professional" who can give a two-hour lecture on "Buy Term and Invest the Difference"?

There's a better way, a simpler way, a more effective way to build your business than by "prospecting" for customers. Read on .....

Who Do You Call On? Who Do You See?

When a rich man says no and a poor man says no the results are the same: no. When a rich man says yes and a poor man says yes the results are quite different.

Scared of dealing with the "upper crust"? Afraid you're being a snob? Not doing your duty? Listen: Your only duty is to make a profit in this business and feed your family. If you do that, you're the greatest American of them all. Don't let anyone try to tell you that you have an "obligation" to serve the masses.

You are a free person.

You are an American.

You have no obligation to anyone except yourself, your family, and the people who trust you. The minute your general agent, manager, or home office starts to work on you to call on the "common folk," tell them to go out and call on them themselves, in person. See how those golden voiced hypocrite react to this type of response. You won't be bothered any more.

Your company would probably love it if you sold only small policies. Face it: small policies are the most profitable for the company ... and the least profitable for you.

So, you call on people who have control of cash flow. Don't call (intentionally) on anyone with a fixed salary or one set by someone else. You're now limited to doctors, lawyers, accountants, dentists, and people who own their own businesses. If salaried people approach YOU for your services, well, by all means help them. Sell the policy ... but don't go after this type of business.

How do you get into the type of business you DO want to go after? Pick out something you find interesting and exciting. Do you like photography? Then become a specialist in solving the insurance problems of that business. Do you like construction? Then become the leader in that market.

Get the industry magazines. Read them, learn about the business. Ask the president of the association to help you define problems his associates have. Ask if you can use his name. Ask who the successful people in the industry are. Now you're rolling ... now you have a chance ... now you can build a great business .....

Because you deal with people in a particular industry, you learn their language, their problems. You learn what they think, how they feel. You know who needs a job, who needs a talent. You have your finger on the pulse of an industry. Calls start coming in to your office. You love your work. You feel important because you ARE important.

If you pick construction, for example, just get one good-sized general contractor on your side. He has, basically, 32 subtrades -- drywall, electrical, and so on -- and gets at least three bids from each trade. He has a half dozen or more subcontractors he's particularly close to. And then there are his suppliers: concrete, finish hardware, lumber, and on and on. He also has an accountant and an attorney ... and they all work closely with him. See the wonderful possibilities? One general contractor is a CAREER! Forget prospecting. Just belly up to the bar on Friday afternoons and meet his friends. They'll be receptive, so have your tools and weapons ready.

This is how you get into the business ... by learning about someone else's business ... by learning to speak their language, understanding their problems, and knowing who's available and who isn't.

So, don't go to the drug store, stand in line at the checkout counter, and try to "prospect." When you're out for an evening and are introduced to someone, don't put him through the "prospecting funnel." Just relax and enjoy the evening. You're not under the gun. You know what you're doing and where you're going.

This doesn't mean that you become so specialized that you turn your back on everyone else. No -- you're a salesperson with a valuable product. You just don't go AFTER everybody you meet. As a result you'll have a good time and let other people have a good time without worrying if you're going to zap them the next day because you met them at a social affair.

If you do meet someone you like and there's some magic between you, of course you're going to call. And, if you're going after the construction market, your contractor will probably introduce you to his friends who aren't contractors, so you'll end up diversifying your business anyway. But you won't have to drive yourself and everyone else nuts going after everyone you meet.

After You've Chosen Your Industry

Here are a couple of ideas you might try once you pick out the industry you want to pursue .....

Take an ad in the industry paper or magazine. Make it a small one with just your name, address, phone number, and the fact that you specialize in solving insurance problems faced by this industry. Keep it there for several years and never change it. You probably won't get a call on the ad, but that's not important. People you do have as customers will see it month after month. Your name is always up there and it's low key.

Attend association meetings, usually held once a month. General contractors have their group, drywall contractors have theirs, and so on. Get to know the president of each association. Take him a good bottle of booze and drop over to his office. Let him know that you work for his people. They usually have door prizes or raffles at these meetings -- make certain you have a gift donated. The bigger you get, the bigger the gift. On election night, you might give away a free trip to Las Vegas. So it costs you a grand ... you'll get it back a hundredfold.

When you go to these meetings, sit with guys you work for. Don't ask anyone for a card. Be low key. Just say hello. Don't tell anyone what you do unless you're asked and then do it matter-of-factly. Just be there month after month, year after year ... things happen. If the association has a guest membership (and they usually do), ask if you can join. Pay your dues on time and respond to any request for fund-raising.

Now isn't this a lot more productive than joining the Chamber of Commerce or the various service organizations with all their diverse activities? You'll find ten insurance people in each of these groups. I doubt you'll find any in trade associations other than fire and casualty folks.

And that's another opportunity. If you join an association and there's a fire and casualty person or two, you'll get to know them after a while. When they find out that you're not after their type of business they'll probably get to know you better and might just give you a few leads. They may even introduce you to their friends.

So you see, you don't have to dial the phone 80 times a day, send out direct mail, or be a pain in the neck to everyone you meet. Here's a simple way of having something going on all the time. And your circles of influence just grow and grow and grow.

Taking It to the Street

The movies and television usually depict the salesman as a pushy, aggressive, self-centered loudmouth, a person to be avoided at all costs.

Like most stereotypes, this picture carries a grain of truth. Do you think this would be such a universally recognized image if it weren't at least partly true?

This image is already imprinted on the minds of our present and potential customers. Let's stop reinforcing it with our own ignorant behavior.

In this section I want you to consider being a business person and not a pushy flake bothering everybody and making them uncomfortable. Also, I want you to get a normal feeling of going to work just like other people do and knowing what you do for a living.

What's Going to Motivate You to Sell?

Financial pressure? I used to think so ... when my bills piled up I'd get off my rear and sell up a storm. As soon as the bills were paid and I had some cash in the bank, I'd sit and look out the window, read, dream up fantastic new proposals, talk with other agents, or make speeches ... everything but sell. A need for money isn't going to do the whole job.

Some managers love to see you in debt. They even hate to see a guy's wife working ... they try to get him to have her quit, hoping that this will put pressure on. It does ... but it's the wrong kind of pressure. When you're under financial pressure you'll do anything, say anything. Oh, you'll get sales ... but you won't be happy ......

Will contests do it? We've already talked about contests. Unless you approach them carefully, all they do is get you to fight for your ego. You'll do it and you'll sell ... but you won't be happy .....

Being number one in your agency? In your region? In your company? Just like the contests. Remember, you ARE number one in YOUR company. Why should you care about being number one in someone else's company? Yes, this goal will cause you to sell, get you to do all those things you shouldn't be doing ... and you won't be happy .....

You will sell effectively and be happy when you're trying to be of value to others, when you feel so strongly about your product and your ideas that you feel guilty if you don't share them with people. You'll never by happy in this business until you come around to this simple concept.

This book could end right here except that so much junk is thrown at you from so many sources that we need to go into it all, in detail, in order for you to start thinking seriously about this concept and -- more importantly -- how you're going to work with it.

How do you get that fantastic feeling inside, way down deep, that makes you unafraid, even eager, to call on people, that makes you feel good for them because they're lucky to meet you?

You must believe in your product and its value. You must believe in the value of the ideas you have. You must believe in the value of your contacts and in your knowledge and experience in helping your customers solve their problems.

How do you "believe in the value of your product"? Simple. You buy it. You own it.

Take this simple test .....

Do you own a minimum of $100,000 of cash value life insurance from your primary company?

Do you have at least $25,000 of permanent cash value life insurance on your spouse?

Do your children have policies guaranteeing them the right to buy at least $100,000 without medical or underwriting requirements at standard rates? Or, do you have $100,000 on each one already?

Do you have all the permanent, non-cancelable disability income protection you can qualify for and need? Forget group. It doesn't count because they can take it away from you. I mean REAL disability income insurance ... do you have it?

Do you have an up-to-date will drafted by an attorney? If you have some bucks, do you have a trust along with it?

Do you have an agreement, in writing, with an agent or manager that clearly states what's to be done with your confidential customer files if you die tonight?

I've asked these questions in cities across the USA and Canada. If there were 300 agents in attendance, five or six could answer all of them "yes." As the size of the audience increased, the numbers went up proportionately. And, when the agents answering "yes" were asked to identify themselves, they were nearly always members of the MDRT who wrote business with major life insurance companies.

What about the hundreds of agents who can't answer "yes"? More than half of the agents I've asked don't own $100,000 of life insurance on their own lives! Can you believe this? If you can't buy $100,000 of cash value life insurance from your primary company because you think it's a bad deal, change companies or quit the business. You will never sell large volumes. Never.

Is your spouse a key person in your life? How can you sell "key man" insurance to others if you don't have insurance on your own spouse? How can you sell estate tax insurance to a man on his wife?

Are you planning for success or failure? Success means you'll have estate taxes ... $100,000 on you and $25,000 on your spouse are the absolute MINIMUMS!

Do you think people have an inherent, guaranteed right to own insurance? Of course not. Can they have it just by writing out a check, with no verification of their medical status? Of course not. Do you have insurance on your children so they WILL be able to buy insurance by just writing a check? No? Then you must think that they can never get sick, get into trouble with the law, smoke dope, or become diabetic ... and you probably aren't much of a tiger closing a sale to an adult either because you probably don't think he could die tonight or have a heart attack tomorrow morning.

Not enough disability income protection or maybe none at all? Are you indestructible? All you have going for you is that big mouth and sweet smile of yours. Lose them and you won't have an income. How long can you last without a paycheck? How can you explain to others what an absolute miracle this insurance is? How can you explain that this is more important than just about any other kind of insurance? That without an income they'll have nothing left to insure after they sell it all to eat and keep a roof over their heads? No wonder you don't sell much .....

No will? Then you're missing the sensation of the business. Pick up the phone, call an attorney, and make an appointment for RIGHT NOW. When they ask, "Why the rush?" say you might die tonight. Go with your spouse and sign the documents.

I always try to sell people on the idea of getting their wills and trusts finished. I make an appointment with a top attorney for them, take them to the office, introduce them to the attorney, and we all sit down together. I've learned so much in these meetings that now I can honestly consider myself quite knowledgeable in estate planning.

Being there with the customers tells them that they are important and builds a solid relationship. After the meeting, take them both out to lunch or dinner and get feedback.

Oh, what about life insurance? When the attorney asks them for a list of assets he has to ask how much life insurance is in force. It becomes real clear that they need more. What an easy sale this is! But you'll never know that until you have your own will and trusts complete.

What about all those customer files in your office? All that confidential information and correspondence? What happens to it all if you flame out on the highway tonight? Do you have a business continuation program? Have you picked out an agent you feel your people would be comfortable with and written a letter of introduction for him?

You haven't? Shame on you! How can you sit across the table from a couple of guys who own a business and talk about a buy-sell agreement if you don't have one yourself?

Sure the home office can come in and take over all your policy ownership cards. Your general agent or manager can divide up your customers and reassign your policies ... but if you have everything in order they won't have to.

I have given my corporate trustee written instructions naming an agent who is to receive $25,000 outright and take charge of my business. He is to protect my renewal income for my heirs, he is to have all new business and my office equipment, and a letter of introduction is to be mailed to every policy holder the day after I die.

Until you folks get all this stuff done I don't feel you'll ever be in the business fully or totally understand the importance of the job you do for people. I've had letters from agents all over the country who've told me that once these things were straight in their own household, they became tigers in the close and could come on strong with a customer in a sincere, inoffensive manner because they had captured the sensation of their business.

What will motivate you to sell? A feeling inside that you are terribly important to people, that you are of great value. That feeling will get you up in the morning even when you have lots of cash in the bank. You might even begin to feel guilty if you don't go to work.

******

Now, isn't this a better concept to run with than winning a contest or being number one in somebody else's company?

Why People Don't Buy Life Insurance

People don't buy life insurance because they don't know the answers to three basic questions: 1) How does it work? 2) Is it the best available? 3) Will it be the best in the future?

At some point during a sales situation, especially if you don't have a strong and solid relationship and a high degree of trust on the part of the customer, your sale will be much simpler if you put these three questions right out on the table .....

"Charlie, you know, most people don't know how how life insurance works. That's one reason they don't pick up the phone and buy what they know they need. Here's an answer for you.

"Charlie, life insurance works. Companies have been around now for over a hundred years, good times and bad. A bunch of wars and major depressions have come and gone. And those old fashioned conservative companies are still going strong.

"And so, Charlie, instead of trying to understand HOW, why don't you just relax and enjoy it? Life insurance works, just like your TV works. You don't know how every tube and transistor does its job and if some technician explained it to you, in about 15 minutes you'd forget what he said or you wouldn't understand it in the first place. So you buy your TV because it says RCA or Panasonic and it goes on when you turn the switch .....

"This policy has Substantial on it. It works. You pay the premium and they give it all back to you with some tax-free profit if you don't die. Or, they pay the face amount to Helen if you do .....

"And Charlie, one other thing. Is this the best policy you can buy? There is no best policy, Charlie. Oh, some agent may tell you different or you might see an ad in a magazine or consumer's report that claims otherwise, but time has a way of evening things out, Charlie. As long as you pick a company that's been around for over a hundred years and has a couple billion in assets, you can't go wrong, now can you?

"What about 10 or 20 years from now, Charlie? You know lots of improvements are made on policies over the years and one nice thing about most major companies is that they pass on these changes to the old policy holders. And the company I represent, Charlie, does just that.

"So now you can relax, Charlie. You know how it works. There is no 'best' company and all changes for the better will be passed along to you. Let's get these papers filled out ....."

To carry this concept a little further .....

Most agents who've talked to Charlie hit him over the head with "how good this stuff is." How refreshing it would be for Charlie to hear an agent say something like this .....

"Charlie, isn't it revolting that because we love someone, and because they'd have a hard time making it if we died tonight, that we have to buy life insurance? Spend dollars that are needed for LIVING NOW on this stuff?

"I hate it, Charlie. I have a million, mostly because I'm too lazy or too busy to follow my own advice and worry about wills, trusts, and estate planning. I have a million on me because I know they'll be able to eat, sleep, and be warm while they weep for me.

"I don't like putting out the money, and just because they'll give it back to me if I don't die, I STILL don't like letting loose of the cash .....

"But one thing, Charlie. Life insurance makes me feel good inside NOW ... WHILE I'M ALIVE! Maybe that's why they call it LIFE insurance. When I get on a plane and fly somewhere and those engines start it down the runway ... I don't have that horrible feeling inside like I haven't done what's right. You know what I mean? If the plane falls out of the sky ... hell, I'd like to be there to watch them spend the dough.

"Anyway, Charlie, you and me, we have the same problem. We don't like the stuff. But, because we LOVE somebody, it's a price we just have to pay. Good thing they give you your money back, right? Hey, let's get the paperwork over with and do something more interesting ....."

You know, folks, I really believe that if we'd stop trying to show people what a "good deal" life insurance is and admit that it's just another thing that grabs our bucks, I think we'd have a much easier time getting people to listen, just a little, and at least they'd know we are straight out folks.

So put away your pads, papers, fancy proposals, and gimmicks and just say "It's the price you have to pay for loving someone" and don't drive the poor customers up the wall trying to shove a "good deal" down their throats. Don't try to show how important YOU are. Don't try to impress the customer with your great knowledge and the beauty of your product so YOU can feel good. That's just ego, folks, just plain ego. All you're supposed to do is get it in force ... NOW. That's your only job.

Why People DO Buy Life Insurance

Because they love someone or something, even if it's just themselves .....

They love someone .....

Just listen to your own heart. Why do you have life insurance? Talk to yourself. See how you feel about your wife or husband ... your little ones ... your not-so-little ones. Feel that great warm feeling you get knowing that if you die tonight, they'll be safe. Their tears will flow but they'll have each other ... and they'll have no fear.

Or something .....

The company, the office, the trucks, the plant, the name on the door, the name on the concrete tiltup, the name on the trucks ... they bled for those things. They lied, they cheated, and yes, sometimes they stole. Only they stole for survival. They fought against overwhelming odds ... the marketplace, competition, government meddling, people who stole from them, bankers with fish eyes who wanted the interest but not the risk, bonding agents who wanted the premium but not the responsibility. They fought them all ... and they won. So they don't let it die just because they're lying in a casket .....

Even if it's just themselves .....

Your customers are million-dollar properties ... no, priceless properties ... and they recognize that fact. Why should they have so much? Just to have it. People like them don't need a reason ... they should have it just to have it.

People buy life insurance for just one reason ... love. Not because of a fancy proposal. Not because of the net cost or fifth dividend. Not because the premium is tax deductible. Not because you're a CLU, MDRT, have a degree, or smell sweet and dress nice and drive the right car .....

Do you hear me? They buy because they love someone or something, even if it's just themselves. Think about this. This is your business: helping people feel good about who and what they love.

When They Say "No, I Don't Want to See You"

First of all, this isn't going to happen too often if you're working the way I've been telling you to work. You'll know so many people from being in all the places where "your" industry hangs out that meeting people won't be a problem.

But someone probably WILL say no someday. What should you do if you really get interested in someone for some reason but when you call they don't want to see you?

Say "Can I call you in a few weeks?" If they say no say "Can I put you on my mailing list and send you some ideas?" If they say no say "Okay, thanks for talking with me" .....

And don't waste any more time on them.

I often wonder why agents spend so much time and agonizing effort trying to see people who don't want to see them .....

Don't you know that there are hundreds of thousands of people, right this minute, who WANT to be called on by an agent for all kinds of reasons? Maybe they've just been to the funeral of a friend or loved one ... or they're planning a long trip ... or they read an article or heard a lecture or saw a story on the news that has made them ready to see an agent .....

Don't listen to managers and other agents who tell you to try to learn all kinds of super-duper techniques aimed at getting an appointment with someone who really doesn't want to see you. Give them your best shot and let them go. It's okay to send some ideas or call in a few weeks to try once again, but don't fight for an appointment.

When you get an appointment, you'll get it because they want to see you ... it's that simple.

So don't feel like a failure or that there's something wrong with you or the product when someone says "No" ..... okay?

When They Say "No, I Don't Want to Buy"

Here's another kind of "No" you're apt to run into eventually .....

Let's say you have a great relationship with Jack. You've sold him policies in the past. You've done the right things at the right time. His business has grown and for one reason or another you're convinced that he not only needs more life insurance but that he can easily afford it.

So you make your presentation. Things are going smoothly, no resistance, and you lean back and say "Jack, let's put this in force. You took the medical, all I need is a check ....."

And he says no.

You try everything. You even ask him to write the check and give it to you, saying that you'll hold it at the office while he thinks things over ... and that if he dies while thinking it over, he'll be covered because you'll turn in the check.

And he says no.

You're exasperated and because of your close relationship you tell him that you just can't understand why he won't at least write the check. He knows you'll give it back to him if he changes his mind. You don't want him walking around one minute without the coverage, especially when he's taken the exam .....

And he still says no.

You know what, folks? He can't tell you or even himself why he's defying your logic and your offer. But the simple fact is this: he's tired of having you, a salesperson, always win. So, all of a sudden, you jump up and say "Jack, I get it. You don't want to buy right now, right?" He says "Yeah, that's what I've been trying to tell you for the last half hour." You say "Okay, tell me 'no' just once more." He says "no" .....

You get up and walk out of his office and close the door. Wait just a few seconds and then walk right back in and say "Jack, how did it feel to win? How did it feel to know that you could tell me no and I'd have to leave, that I couldn't win this one? How did it feel, Jack?"

He looks puzzled and says "I don't know what you're talking about." You say "Well, Jack, we've been doing business for six years now and you've bought everything I've suggested to you because deep down you know it's good for you and does a job you need done. But now you're tired of seeing me win every time, so you said no and I left. But what you won is nothing,

nothing at all. And if you're wrong and you lose the gamble, you lose a half million dollars for your family. Come on, Jack, is winning so important? Give me a check ....."

And he will!

When They Want to Cancel the Policy

When people want to cancel an insurance policy, they usually just call the general agency or mail in a request. They don't contact you because they're afraid of you and deep down they know that something is wrong. Oh, sometimes they'll call but most of the time you get the word from the general agency that a policy is overdue or that a request for cancellation has been sent it.

So you give the customer a call and say .....

"Hi, Mike. Hey! Why didn't you give me a call? It's no bother, I'll bring the forms right over and get you a check for your cash value. No need for me to mail them and have you wait an extra five days. I'll be happy to stop by. Can I come now?"

Over you go. You walk into the business office or home and pull out the papers. They're filled out with the policy number and you have the cash value figures on a piece of paper. You tell him that as soon as he signs the form, you'll be back with a check in a day or so.

Now that you've assured him by your actions that you're not a threat and that you're not going to try and talk him out of anything, you've got a customer who's terribly off balance. He'll probably start to tell you WHY he's canceling his policy. Hold up your hand and say "Hey, it's your money. I told you if nothing happens you'd get all or most of your money back depending on how long you kept the policy. You don't have to explain anything to me. There must be a real important problem you're trying to solve and I don't want to add to your problems by making you feel uncomfortable. I'm on your side ... I know that you know what you're doing ....."

Then what? Here are two concepts you might want to try after tailoring them to your individual selling style. The simple one first .....

Say "Would you mind if I buy your policy from you? I'll give you my personal check for the exact surrender value of the policy if you'll just sign these change of ownership forms ....."

He'll ask why you want the policy .....

"Well, it doesn't cost any more money for your policy. You've had it well over a year now and all the costs are paid. If you don't want to pay more premiums you don't have to ... the policy will carry itself for years with very small payments, and since I know you are definitely going to die someday, it's a good long term investment for MY FAMILY. Oh, one more thing. I can get the cash out of the policy and cover almost all of the check I'm going to give you and still not have to pay very much to keep it in force. It's only fair to tell you about these options in case you want to keep it. If not, let me buy it."

Guess what ... he won't let you buy it from him and he won't cancel the policy!

Concept number two works in business and personal situations. You go through the cancellation process and when you have the papers ready for signature you say .....

"Mike, will you do me a small favor? Ask your secretary to bring in one of your big accounts payables, an actual bill your company is going to pay this month? Just go along with me for a minute."

In comes the bill from U.S. Steel for $23,000 for pipe that was bought and put in the ground last month. "When are you going to pay this bill, Mike?" He says "in a few days so we can get the discount for prompt payment. Besides, we have a reputation for paying promptly and that's good for our credit line."

"Mike, you don't want to pay my company $6,000 for this life insurance premium. You don't want to pay it because you're short of cash right now. But you're going to pay this $23,000 bill to U.S. Steel. Mike, let's say you're going down the highway tonight and some idiot weaves across the center line, plows into you, and moves you into a concrete casket .....

"We go to the president of U.S. Steel and tell him that you wanted to keep your credit good so you paid the $23,000 bill instead of giving a life insurance company $6,000. And now we want U.S. Steel to give Mary $200,000 tax-free and never demand repayment so she can clean up all the stuff you left undone. The president of U.S. Steel will throw us out of his office. U.S. Steel doesn't care about Mary or your kids ... but WE DO!"

At this point, pick up the invoice, tear it in half, roll it into a ball, and throw it on the floor. "Come on, Mike, get your priorities straight!!! Give me $6,000 and pay U.S. Steel $17,000 and catch up later. No, don't bother, I'll fix up this invoice and give your bookkeeper an invoice for $6,000 and pick up the check this afternoon."

You can do the same thing in personal insurance. It could be a car payment, a doctor bill, or whatever. Just get their priorities in line and the value of our great product where it belongs -- in front of all those other people who'll have their hands out when your customer is in the ground .....

Joint Work

Remember when you were a kid playing baseball? .....

It's the bottom of the ninth with two outs. The bases are loaded and your team is behind one run. It's your turn to go to the plate. On the way up to the batter's box your stomach is in knots ... fear of the unknown ... fear of failure. Suddenly the coach yells out "Hey Kid! Wait a minute, come back here! I want Pat to bat for you!"

Tears fill your eyes. No matter how Pat does at the plate, no matter what the team does, no matter who wins, you can't share in either the joy or the agony. You didn't go up to bat.

So it is with joint work, for the new agent. Far too often managers encourage new agents or agents just barely scraping by to tag along with an "old pro" ... split cases ... go be the "bird dog" until you somehow learn how to do it by watching.

Forget it. You need time at bats. You need to experience the victories and the failures. If you're short on knowledge, start reading and get the facts. If you don't know what to read, ask the old pro. THEN go out there in the field and do it.

I didn't do joint work until I had well over 50 million in force. I didn't take any old pros out with me until I knew how to sell. Then, when I did take an old pro or a technician out in the field, I knew what was going on. The subtle things they did were crystal clear. I learned and I'm still learning.

As a novice, you most likely won't be aware of an old pro's skills or what those skills are. And, when the sale is made, you'll be apt to have a bad taste in your mouth and say, "I could have done that! And now I have to split the commission!" You probably won't even recognize the pro's value.

If you want some help, why not offer an experienced agent 10% of a case to go over the facts and figures, find an approach, and rehearse the sales idea and presentation with you? Then, if you win or lose, come back and go over the events with him.

This way, you'll be learning and it'll be a good experience for you. You won't have tears in your eyes like the little kid who didn't get the chance to feel the crack of the bat hitting the ball, hear the cheer of the crowd, or feel the flush as third base blazes past.

The joy of life is in experiencing it ... in being a player, not a spectator.

Replacing Policies

When I first came into this business I was with a top-line mutual company that stressed to its agents the value of its low net cost. In no way was replacement encouraged but this company's exceptional cost advantages were pushed so hard that my natural tendency to seek the line of least resistance prevailed.

My first year in the business all I'd do was go into a contractor I knew from my former career in construction and ask if I could give him a "bid" on his life insurance. He'd never heard that one before. I'd tell him that there was a tremendous difference in cost from one company to another and that if he'd let me see his policies I probably could save him a small fortune.

In almost every case I was able, one way or another, to show him that I could improve the quality of his coverage and since he usually bought life insurance from a casualty agent working through one of the stock companies, I was rarely if ever challenged by another agent.

Then too ... being a former contractor I felt that rules were for others. I didn't fill out the required replacement forms because I thought they were a waste of time. I usually answered the questions regarding replacement "no," using the mental justification that I wasn't going to replace the policy just then, at the time the application was taken ... I'd replace it if my company issued a policy. Or, I'd convince the contractor to "minimum deposit" his policy -- to pay just enough to keep it in force -- by telling him not to dump more money into such junk.

I went around my community with big Home Office letters emblazoned on my forehead. Any agent from another company was, in my opinion, either ignorant or a thief because he didn't represent the "very best" company in the business. I made a total ass out of myself at life underwriter meetings by actually stating these opinions out loud.

And then came my first death claim .....

My "very best" company would not insure this customer. A well-known Canadian company did. He died 11 months later, 6 months after the controller of the same company died. My "very best" company was not on the risk, was not the company that had issued the policy -- this same Canadian company was. And here I had yelled and screamed at the agents working for this Canadian company for almost two years, calling them whores and prostitutes and asking how they could sell such junk. After the second death I went to the manager of the Canadian company with tears in my eyes and apologized. I had finally realized who the "very best" company was ... the company on the risk at death.

After almost four years in the business I went to my first MDRT meeting. I had qualified earlier but my general agent thought I'd be better off not going to MDRT meetings, that I should just go to home office and regional company conventions so I wouldn't mingle with the whores and prostitutes. He never came out and said that, of course, but other folks in the agency and I had that feeling and went along with the "esprit de corps" that helped us survive those first few years in the business.

It was at the 1974 MDRT meeting, my first, that I actually met agents from other companies. As the days went by I soon forgot to ask what company people worked with ... it didn't seem to matter. I soon made lasting friendships with fantastic agents from all over the country. My mind exploded with new ideas and concepts. I was coming out of a prison, a self-imposed prison.

These folks were not whores and prostitutes, they were magnificent, loving, caring human beings who loved this business and who served their customers in countless areas beyond just selling them a policy.

And then there was the time a guy's wife lied to me .....

I was hungry for sales. It was contest time and I was hitting everything that walked so I could be one of the "top ten in the West!"

I insured a guy and sent home an application for his wife to sign. She did and the policy was issued. Later, a claim was filed ... and the company denied payment because a check on medical records indicated that she had been sick for a long time and the information wasn't on the application. She lied because she never told her husband that she had been so sick before they got married.

The family sued me and we settled out of court. It taught me the value of the one- or two-year incontestability clause in old policies. I almost lost my right to earn a living and be a part of this great business over a lousy sale .....

The upshot of all this is that I don't replace policies any more unless there's a very, very serious reason for doing so. An agent just like me, with the same fears and frustrations, got up one day and went through the process of helping people realize their importance to their loved ones. Besides, after the first or second premium has been paid on a policy, it takes years for any new one, no matter how competitive, to catch up.

Replacement is dangerous, for you and for your customers. I cannot emphasize this point too strongly. Even if there are no pre-existing conditions and the policy in force might cost a little more IF your company comes through the way it says it will, how about their attitude toward our industry in general and you the agent in particular? Why should they trust you more than they trusted the agent who sold them the "garbage"? And just how important is the extra money they might get in 10 or 20 years?

These are judgment calls, my friends, but let me tell you from experience: don't replace. Be a builder, not a destroyer. Build on the foundation laid by another agent just like you, who was sincere and dedicated to putting a policy in force on a person who loved someone or something.

Rated Cases

Try to work with a company that doesn't issue too many rated cases.

I'm serious. My customers are the walking wounded and they hate to take medicals. My average customer is 58 years old, has half a stomach and high blood pressure, is overweight, and doesn't exercise except for elbow-bending.

So, I went with a company that will use its imagination to give them standard policies. If this sounds like a plug, it isn't ... I don't want you in my company, the Mutual Benefit. If every agent started joining we'd be all through ... we can barely handle the business now. So just read this and try to get your company to fire its president and chairman of the board and put in a great salesman and tough high school dropout ex-Marine as chairman and then ask them to get you stuff to sell .....

My company puts a sick person with one or two (or however many it takes) healthy folks and gives each of them a standard contract based on some kind of figuring. (Remember I didn't take CLU so I don't know how they figure this out.) I take a 5% cut in first year commission and the first nine years of dividends are cut on the policies since this business is put in a "pool."

The end result is that they all get standard policies, including the sick one. I've checked it out -- it comes out to be about the same net cost as if the sick one had been rated individually and the others received standard policies ... but not always ... sometimes they get a better deal. Besides, there's something heart-warming about getting someone who's sick a standard policy .....

And then we have a mini-pool. We can write $50,000 non-medical with only four or five questions like "Have you had cancer or heart problems?" and "What is your height? Your weight?" These are guaranteed issue (just about) and come back standard in about three weeks. They'll take up to about four sick folks and still issue standard but we have to feed in healthy people too, like spouses who don't want to go for an exam and busy folks who could care less about dividends when they're worth a thousand bucks an hour or more.

Also, we can write non-medical up to $150,000 to age 40, $100,000 to age 60, and $50,000 to age 65 just by filling out the everyday non-med form with all the questions. Again, this saves time and gets insurance in force with a minimum of problems.

I can just hear the "purists," the "ethical nuts" screaming about cutting the dividends and so on. These people aren't worth taking time or space explaining this or arguing about it. They can go back to their black and white offices and pound their heads. I'll just go out and put insurance in force on people who might die in the next few minutes and leave the ethics to God. He had to deal with nitpickers who wanted to know why He cured people on the Sabbath. I have great faith that He will understand even if "they" don't.

The sad fact is, folks, you can't all work for companies that have "pools" and bundle underwriting. So, try this on for size. Work this over in your minds and see if you can buy the concept yourself before you try selling it.

There is no such thing as a rated case.

Companies come out with only two types of offers. A policy with a premium that can be put in force and a decline. A decline means the customer has no life expectancy, none.

Say Harry is 45 and the premium in your rate book says it's $2,500 for whole life. If the company issues a policy for $3,500, they haven't issued a rated or substandard case. Look in the rate book. What age has a $3,500 rate for a hundred thousand? Maybe it's age 52. Let's say it is. You show Harry the rate book. Show him age 52. Tell him the company issued a standard policy for a man aged 52. He has run his body down to the point where he has lived on earth 45 years but he has run so hard he's actually 52.

Tell him that seven years is not such a bad price to pay for all he has achieved. Tell him that you know guys who would trade 10, 15, maybe 20 years to have accomplished what he has and to have had the experiences he's had. Tell him there's a price we all pay for success and achievement.

Next, tell him that if he'll eat better food, lose some weight, get his blood pressure back to normal, cut down on the booze, and take a vacation once in a while, the company will give him back a few years. If he works as hard now to get himself back in shape as he did to build his business, maybe he can be 46 next year.

And then congratulate him on getting the policy and get his check.

There is no such thing as a rated case .....

Kickbacks ("Consulting Fees")

Are your hands trembling as you hold this page? Are you ready for this? Take heart, dear soul, it'll be over quickly.

There are basically two kinds of kickbacks. (No use trying to soften what they are with another name.) First, there are those you give directly to someone who just bought insurance, either as a bribe or because for one or more reasons you want to. The second kind is a bribe you give to someone who helps you get business by referring you to people or who is in a position to help you help a customer make a favorable decision.

I've done both. Not because I'm a crook, but rather because I'm a good practical businessman who will do the things he feels he must do to survive and make a profit.

The few times I paid a first month's premium for a guy or gave away a chunk of my commission, I was in a contest or a financial bind. Each and every time it created serious problems in future relationships.

The few times I sent "consultant's fees" to people who gave me leads actually led to my no longer having relationships with them. I made them prostitutes and I was the pimp. I was just getting started, I was hungry, and I didn't know what I was doing. But: I'd do it again. Some of my biggest customers and dearest friends were referrals I paid for in one way or another. Not all of you are forturnate enough to work with a company that has solved to any great extent the problem of rated cases. Here's where I feel kickbacks may have some merit and are worthy of consideration. Here are my feelings on the matter and they haven't changed since the day I came into this business .....

On a rated case, the agent shouldn't receive any commission on the extra cost. None. It's bad enough to hit a guy for additional bucks because of his problem but for the agent to actually earn more money on it is despicable and I think this industry is rotten to do it.

When I get rated cases I sometimes help the folks out, even if they don't ask. I don't always give them my commission directly ... sometimes I do some extra work that I don't have to ... once I sold a car to a guy's son for half what it was worth. There are times when I just can't take a sick person's hard-earned money on a heavy rating, and I personally bless you with good wishes if you don't either.

What do you do when someone just out and asks for some of your commission? It depends on what kind of financial shape

____

you're in. If you're dirt broke, don't be proud -- take what you can get and run. The trouble here is that it can become a habit and you'll soon leave the business or be thrown out of it. The main thing is to try to avoid giving this turkey your commission by any means you can.

For example, try saying "I only get 15% on this type of policy because it has such high early cash value." Phoenix Mutual has a commission schedule in its brokerage contract. Go get one. You'll see that Ordinary Life Special (a graded premium product) pays only 40% the first year and 10% after in renewals. They have a very high cash value policy that pays only 25% the first year. Their other products have the normal 55% commission and 5% in renewals.

If you get stuck, whip one of these out to show the difference in commissions that various companies pay. They probably read a "consumer" report that said you get 55% on whole life and 35% on term. This will blow that out of the water or at least create doubts. It's worth a try with these creeps, and although you'll probably still have to kickback, it might be a lot less.

You'll run into some cases where customers are really down. They need coverage and it looks like they might pull themselves out. Don't be afraid to invest (I said invest, not kickback). Pay a couple of months if you believe in them. If they get on their feet don't take it back unless they jam it at you. If it works out you may have friends for life .....

I had a contractor who was down and I mean down. I paid his premium for a year without telling him about it. Sure enough a development came in big. He called and said he wanted to have some life insurance again now that he could afford it. I told him I'd be right down. I brought him his policy with the premium receipts ... tears rolled down his face. He's one of my closest friends now and a big booster. He never seems to tire of telling people about what I did .....

I'm a big boy. I'll make good decisions just like any other good businessman. But don't ever change that anti-rebate law. It protects all of us and our industry.

Don't put yourself into a box. Make these decisions one at a time, day by day. No need to say "I'll never give up any of my commission!" Why take a position you may have to defend one day?

Life isn't a neat set of rules. You go out there and do the best you can day after day. That's all. Keep in mind, though, that the rules this industry has set up are the result of many

---

years of trial and error. When you break them you're probably going to get burned somehow, some way. Just don't beat yourself to death or feel that you are alone with your problems ... or that this is a rotten business.

And don't try to cop out by thinking (and maybe saying) "In order to be a big producer you have to be a crook." Not so ... just sometimes.

Public Relations

The term "public relations" actually describes a properly used kickback.

Sending good customers or centers of influence on junkets is smart business and is more of an investment than anything else. People who don't ask for anything go bananas when you pick up the phone and say .....

"You mean a lot to me. Without your help I'd never have been so successful this year. I want to share my happiness with you. You haven't taken any time off lately and I want you and your wife to get away and relax. You'll have two tickets to Acapulco and all expenses except booze for four days. You leave at noon next Thursday."

What a glow you get inside! Nobody has ever done that for him! You bind yourself to him in an honest and sincere way without making him feel like a prostitute.

And then there is the wonderful world of entertainment. Get tickets to ball games and take your customers or just send them. Do lots of things with them. Go to plays together. Go to dinner together. When the check comes pick it up. (They'll probably insist on splitting it with you.)

Pretty soon you'll start to get phone calls inviting you to go with them to their grand affairs and you'll be seen at the right places by the people you want to deal with directly or who will one day influence your customers favorably when your name is mentioned.

What Do You Have to Sell?

Ideas!
Concepts!
Here are a whole bunch of them .....

Super Star Contracts ... Estate Tax Bonds ... Tax Exempt Corporate Trusts ... Clean Up the Mess Funds ... Buy Out Your Partner With Tax Deductible Dollars ... Buy Another Business With Tax Deductible Dollars ... Golden Handcuffs ... King (or Queeen) of the Sick Ones ... King (or Queen) of the Kids .....

Ideas, ideas, ideas ... sell ideas ... sell concepts.

The Super Star Contract is covered in my 1977 MDRT speech called "Just a Salesman," reprinted in the Appendix. This speech also talks about selling disability protection and saving your customers' businesses if their spouses die.

Estate Tax Bonds .....

"You know, Charlie, when you die the feds will come in, dig you up nine months later, and pick your bones clean of any flesh left on them. They call this collecting death taxes. Charlie, you know about death taxes. If you want to know approximately what you'll have to pay when either you or your wife dies, just add up what you've got ... take your time ... got the number? Okay, now divide by 2 ... got that one? Now take 30%. That's the minimum you'll have to pay if you spend the rest of your waking moments sitting in lawyers' offices dotting every "i" and crossing every "t" in a will and trust they draw up for you .....

"Charlie, I sell estate tax bonds. You pay a small premium each year for the bond, just like you do in construction, Charlie ... and when you or your wife dies, my company turns the bond over to the tax collectors and refunds all or most of the premiums they collected. Oh, and when you pay those bond premiums, Charlie, you can list them as assets on your corporate balance sheet (as "cash value, life insurance") and that helps your "net quick" (liquid assets) for bonding.

"I've sold a lot of estate tax bonds to contractors, Charlie. They don't want any life insurance but they do want a bond covering their estate tax liability" .....

Tax Exempt Corporate Trusts cover the whole field of retirement programs including profit sharing and pensions. When a corporation sets up a retirement program they're really setting

---

up a tax exempt corporate trust. They take a tax deduction when they make a contribution. The trust can invest the money and the earnings are tax-free. Very few people want retirement programs because they don't understand them, but they all like tax exempt corporate trusts.

"Charlie, I sell "Clean Up the Mess" programs for contractors. Do you want one? What is it? Well, you have a lot of things going that not everyone knows about. There are lots of things in your head that aren't written down too well, Charlie.

"As long as you're alive, it's okay, but if you die, your business and your family are going to need some extra bucks to "Clean Up the Mess" you've left around town.

"Charlie, look ... you're 50 years old. If you give me a check for about three grand, just one time, I'll set up a $100,000 tax-free "Clean Up the Mess" program for you. That's all my company will charge: three grand just once.

"Oh, they'll send you a bill for three grand each year ... but you don't have to pay it. If you do pay it, you can have it back any time you want it. If you don't pay it, they'll charge you eight percent deductible interest on the three grand. You always have a choice. Or, Charlie, if you don't want to pay for it all and get it over with, my company will let you pay it off over ten years starting at about $700 this year.

"Look, I'm not going to go into detail about this. You have the concept, you can figure out the rest" .....

(See how attractively term with a retro conversion in ten years can be presented?)

Buy Your Partner Out With Tax Deductible Dollars .....

There are all kinds of ways. The customer can set up a stock contribution plan (retirement) where the corporation contributes cash to a retirement program and the retirement fund buys the stock of the partner ... ESOT .....

The customer could set up a defined benefit pension plan, make the cash contribution, borrow out of his vested interest, and buy the stock of his partner. Pay himself interest back into the plan, and later repay the loan by transferring some real property back to the pension plan when it's ready to be fully funded .....

"Golden Handcuffs" ... another variation of deferred compensation just like the Super Start Contract. Read about it in the 1977 MDRT proceedings.

King (or Queen) of the Sick Ones .....

Tell people that you specialize in selling life insurance to people who are very sick or who are dying. Work with a good substandard broker and go after this business. Learn how to layer on group insurance which will include someone who has really had it if you insure enough people. This is a great business to look into and you won't have much resistance. People who are sick and dying will buy all you can get them .....

King (or Queen) of Kids .....

Tell people that you specialize in "taking the fear out of the future of little children." Sell simple juvenile packages. Call up the president of a company after you find out the name of his son and say "I want to talk to you about your son, Robert. I want to show you how to take the fear out of his future."

Go in and sell him a million on his son ... or a hundred thousand or ten. Just show him a ledger statement. Tell him he doesn't have to give his money to Robert. He can always keep the cash value but "look what a great deal this will be for him, especially with waiver of premium on it. Why, if Robert were ever to become disabled he'd have a tax-free income from his policy via cash values and dividends for life!

"And, if Robert is ever caught smoking dope, gets picked up for drunk driving, or decides to be a dynamite blaster, he has a fantastic program to protect your grandchildren and assure you that if he dies, you won't have to start raising kids all over again" .....

******

These are the types of ideas that get a customer interested in you, not a demonstration of "buy term and invest the difference."

Ideas ..... ideas ..... ideas ..... sell ideas .....

Par or Non-Par?

Which is better, participating insurance which pays the policy holder dividends or non-participating insurance? The answer? YES! Which is better, a stock company or a mutual company? The answer? YES! The best policy, the best company, is the one on the risk at death. If I were selling a stock company product, my attitude would be:

> "Look, Mr. Customer, if you want dividends, go buy IBM or AT&T. I sell guarantees, not projections into the future."

If I were selling a mutual company product, my attitude would be:

> "Look, Mr. Customer, what's wrong with having a chance to share in the profits of a major life insurance company? They have a very good track record and usually outperform their projections. As in any other investment, if you share in the profits you share in the risk. But I think you'll agree that the risk is very small -- the majority of values illustrated here are guaranteed."

You see, folks, there is no "right" way. There is no black and white. During the Depression most mutual companies had trouble paying dividends and nearly all of them reduced the scale. Who knows what would have happened if World War II hadn't started .....

Personally, I like to sell a top-line mutual because I like the hedge the dividends give me against inflation, especially if it's a well-run company with a solid investment portfolio that has stood the test of time. But: I'd have no hesitation about selling a quality stock company product as long as contractual improvements were passed along to old policy holders.

Your problem is not worrying about what's "best" but rather learning how to sell what you already have. Put aside all the baloney that a company and its management will throw at you while you're getting your business established. This is just one more area where they can trip you up with more distractions.

You won't be bothered by this if you stay away from the general agency and home office conventions. You won't find much of this talk going on among top agents, and this topic hardly ever comes up at the Million Dollar Round Table.

Net Cost

What is net cost? Some would say it's the cash value and dividend deducted from the premiums paid.

I say it's mental gymnastics performed by general agents competing for people to sell for them rather than for the other guy. These sad folks tear up our brains with their endless debate over "who's the best" while completely ignoring the fact that most of them are simply incompetent salespeople.

There's an argument that simply stated says that if net cost isn't important, you should sell just term insurance, that if cash values, dividends, and paid up values have no importance, why do you bother selling whole life?

Again, the proponents of this argument are assuming that the proposed insured has ANY life insurance. Since the folks who start these arguments have rarely, if ever, sold a single policy, the whole subject should be dismissed.

Stop selling cash values. Start selling life insurance. All whole life does is offer a level premium throughout the lifetime of the insured. The fact that there are ANY cash values is a gift ... a darned wonderful gift. In fact, it's a wonder it can be done at all.

So, to wrap up this debate, just don't get into it with anyone. It's a waste of time and distracts from your main objective: putting life insurance in force on human beings whose deaths would cause economic problems for the people they love.

(And think of all the millions of dollars that home offices can save if they'll stop trying to force feed us all this garbage!)

Term Insurance

Why are you so afraid of term insurance? Why is so much time and energy spent trying to show how lousy this stuff is when it's so great?

You know why? Because the premium is low and the commission is usually 20% lower than for whole life (35% vs. 55%).

Term insurance is the best product in your sales bag ... if you sell the right kind of term insurance. I mean the kind that converts into a whole life product that you would buy if you had the money ... the kind that allows you to keep it for a minimum of three and preferably ten years and then make an optional original age conversion with full credit for all the premiums paid ... the kind that has a waiver of premium that allows your customers to upgrade their policies to a whole life product if they become disabled, with the company paying the whole life premium, not just the term coverage, giving them a built-in disability policy because the dividends and cash values accumulate tax-free and are available .....

Let's face it. Companies usually give you half the credit (and sometimes less) in their games and contests for a term policy. You sell $100,000 of term and they tell you that you only get "credited" for $50,000 in the contest or the monthly agency bulletin. Tell that to the widow when you bring her a check for $100,000. The blasted hypocrites! I hate, and I mean HATE, this aspect of our business because it encourages agents to put their own interests and egos ahead of what's best for their customers. Until this practice is changed, the industry, in my opinion, is just plain dishonest!

Your job is to put death protection in force. The widow doesn't care if its term, shmerm, or whatever. She doesn't care if it's Prudential or "Shifting Sands of Arizona." She just wants to see the amount on the check!

Now that THAT's over with, let's get on with this discussion in a calmer manner .....

What would happen if all you could sell was term insurance on the initial sale? Come on, consider this hypothetical situation, don't run from it. What would be your fate if you could sell just term insurance and hope you could trade it in later?

Let's check it out. Let's say the average guy you sell is 35 years old. You sell him a $100,000 term policy with waiver of premium and accidental death. The premium in a quality company offering all the proper "goodies" will be about $30 a month or $360 annual. You get 35% of that for about 120 bucks.

How hard would it be to sell just one a day, five days a week for 48 weeks? Not very hard because you wouldn't sell just $100,000. You'd sell what the customer needs ... $150,000, $200,000, whatever ... and you wouldn't have all that resistance to fight.

Your customers would know that over the years they'd have the option of trading up. You'd know that it's easier to talk to them about improving the "quality" of their programs than it is to talk them into buying more.

They would know that they would have ten years or more to get their money back on original age conversions and they'd feel very comfortable with that. Further, if they made original age conversions back to the day they bought their policies, the company would credit most of the premiums they paid toward the new policies. They wouldn't feel like they were throwing money down a sewer, would they?

Accountants and attorneys would love you. In fact, you'd actually start to hear your customers and their advisors say "I don't know about buying term insurance. How much would whole life be?" Honest, it would happen.

You'd build up a backlog of future business that would drive you nuts if you knew what the years ahead would bring.

But wait a minute! You wouldn't win any contests!

You might not even qualify for the Million Dollar Round Table the first year you try this ... but around the second or third you'd be in the FIVE Million Dollar Club, better known as the "Top of the Table."

You see, folks, the "system" we all live with nowadays is at fault. There's no ego reward for selling term and they mislead you into thinking you can't make ends meet.

Even my beloved MDRT adds to the problem, and I'm at a loss for the solution unless they were to change the entry level to $10,000,000 of death protection regardless of what type it is. That sure would get everyone out selling term, wouldn't it?

Hope you'll give this some thought and try it .....

Love term ... love term ... it's beautiful stuff, if you don't play the ego game and try to win the contests.

Some Tips on Selling Term Insurance

You'd be surprised how easy it is to sell $100,000 of term for $25 or $30 bucks a month today, especially if you remember what I've been telling you throughout this book: life insurance is already sold. You don't have to tell anyone how good it is. All they want to know is how to pay for it. So make it easy on them ... get that first sale.

Try saying that term insurance is like putting up the structural steel framework in a 100-story building. Later, as you begin to lease out the property, you begin to fill in and finish the floors (that is, trade up to permanent insurance in stages).

And don't say "let's convert." Say "let's trade in your term insurance while it still has trade-in value." You don't convert your used car, do you? Don't you trade it in? Let's start using language people understand for a change.

Remember, the older people get, the more conservative they usually become. The word "saving" is no longer a dirty word and the phrase "forced savings" has appeal as they look back at the years they worked, the money they made, and how little they put away. And there you are with your term product in force and ready to improve the "quality" of their programs and not the "quantity" .....

Suppose a customer says he can buy a cheaper term product than the one your company offers. It's from some low-cost outfit and converts into garbage but he still insists on getting the cheap stuff. Just say "Look, if you want garbage, go deal with a garbage man" and walk out. He isn't going to be worth your valuable time .....

Here's another approach that takes advantage of numbers. If you try this technique, be certain that you really understand how whole life works, that you've bought plenty of it yourself, and that you understand that in the long run, whole life is a darned good buy and superior to term if you can afford the cash flow.

Tell your customers that term costs only $30 a month for $100,000. They say they want to buy so you write the application. Ask if they're really saving any money. Ask with a smile. They'll probably admit that they aren't, so you say .....

"Look, Charlie ... you're giving me $30. If you put another $110 with it, here's what will happen. You're giving the insurance company extra money they don't need to insure you ... all they need is the $30. So, they take this money and they do a good job of investing it. And the government gives insurance companies tax breaks that banks and savings and loans don't get.

"So, if you give them an extra $110 along with the $30, Charlie, they'll give you your $30 back. They'll make enough money on the $110 to pay the cost of your insurance. Charlie, where can you get $30 a month return for $110? Can you afford to put the $110 away?

"And remember, after a year you can switch back and forth ... pay $30 when you're short and then put away $110 when you get fat again. You have flexibility. Let's do it ... you can at least save the $110 for a year, can't you? ....."

And then work with your customers. Sell a good policy with good first year cash value and dividends. After that they really are getting their money back. The insurance costs only the interest they would have made if they had put the whole thing in the bank. But, they might die and if they do they need the insurance so it's better to give their savings to the insurance company than to a bank. They get a much better return .....

And that's a good way to trade in the term year by year.

Love term ... sell the daylights out of it.

Building Relationships (and Your Business)

Before you can build healthy relationships with others, you must first build a healthy relationship with yourself. Yes, you've heard all this before, but it bears repeating. Only when you accept yourself as you are can you begin to build those long-term relationships that bring you easy sales year after year.

Start with your insecurity about money. Do you see why it's mandatory that your financial affairs be in order if you're going to pursue a career in sales? The most effective way I know to straighten out your finances is to stop buying things you don't really need, stuff you buy just to make you feel good.

Next, tackle all those other things you do just for self-gratification, to sooth your ego, escape from your problems, ease the pressure, hide your fears and anxieties, cover your pain ....

If you seek excitement for its own sake, recognize that it's only a method of forgeting about your problems for a while. Ditto for escaping into your favorite fantasies .....

If you smoke, stop. Smoking is just another form of self-gratification used to ease the pressure ... and it's a form that can kill you. Is that any way to treat a friend, your best friend (YOU)? Same with booze and mind-altering drugs .....

Eliminate gratuitous sex, the kind where you use your partner for your own self-gratification .....

Stop seeking power over people in your pursuit of the illusion of being in control of your own destiny .....

Above all, establish (or re-establish) a strong, loving relationship with your Creator .....

(All this advice, by the way, is to help you improve your relationship with yourself, not to make you a monk or saint.)

What don't you like about yourself? Change it! Take ACTION! Write down your fears, write down your anger. Touch base with those feelings. Face the pain you're trying to cover over with smoking, drinking, drugging, excitement, fantasies, meaningless sex, loud music, buying things, wielding power over people, compulsive working, and constant activity ... whatever device you've been using. Get your life in order.

When you treat yourself right, you can build relationships with others and sell with confidence. Why? Because when you have self-respect you can treat others with respect. Simple!

Recruiting

If I were a general agent .....

I'd first of all consider myself a very special insurance salesman. I'd be selling life insurance THROUGH my agents. They would enable me to do hundred of millions of dollars in sales instead of the amount I could do selling to consumers one at a time.

Working from this basic concept, I'd recruit potential agents from industries that interested me (construction, in my case).

The entire emphasis of the agency would be to serve the construction industry. If I inherited agents from a prior general agent I'd guide them into an industry of their own choosing -- medicine, automobile repair shops, whatever. BUT: I'd do my recruiting within the industry I enjoyed most.

As general agent, I'd be the one to join the trade associations at first. Instead of looking for life insurance prospects I'd be looking for agent candidates. I'd let everyone I met know that my general agency specialized in the construction industry and that I was looking for top people to join me.

At the meetings there'd be manufacturers' reps who attend to meet the contractors who buy their materials or the architects who specify their products. These people would be my first choice. They'd have a rapport with people in the industry; they'd know who was who and who was doing what.

The agency office would be furnished with a theme emphasizing construction. There'd be pictures of great projects completed by our customers instead of "man of the month" photos of agents. We'd have a nice rec room that could double as a conference room with a bar, big TV screen, and so on. Agents could bring contractors up for Monday night football games with free beer and hot dogs. We'd throw an annual $100,000 golf open for all the contractors and their employees with at least that much in force on their lives. We'd do that instead of spending money going to the home office annual meeting .....

Soon the word would be out and recruiting would start to come naturally. The agency would take on character and become well-known in the circles of influence within the construction industry .....

See how this approach would simplify recruiting? It would also get agents away from the horrible thought of having to "prospect" every minute and driving everyone they meet socially nuts by putting them through a "funnel."

If only I had the patience to wetnurse new agents and put up with home office baloney and agents who come in drunk or pregnant and all the other nightmares a general agent goes through .....

At least it's something for you folks out there in general agent land to think about .....

Fact Finders

Other than getting people bank loans they couldn't have gotten without your help, I don't know of any better way to build a relationship than sitting down for a half an hour or so and filling out a fact finder form. Just about any of the fact finders put out by the home office will do ... better yet, design one yourself.

Remember, the reason people do business with you is NOT because you have the best product, service, or prices ... they do business with you because they feel you understand them. And what better way to give this feeling than by sitting down, asking questions, and carefully recording the answers? It begins to build ideas in the customers' minds. They start thinking about things they've put in the back of their minds ... things like "What happens when I die?"

Basically, you want to know how they feel about insurance. Ask just a few old-fashioned questions .....

> Do you own any life insurance?
> Why did you buy it?
> What don't you like about it?
> What do you like about it?
> Why would you buy more?

I wish I'd remember to ask these questions more often. Most of the time I forget. I manage to get the policy sold somehow, but when I do ask those questions I have an easier time. They're your hammer and nails ... your basic tools.

Here's an in-depth interview .....

> Do you have an up-to-date will? Do you want one? Leave it to me .....
> What's going to happen to your business if you die tonight? You're not certain? What would you like to happen? Do you really want that to happen? Leave it to me .....

Here's a relationship-building interview based on just one question:

> What really scares the daylights out of you?

Or a little softer:

What's your biggest problem right now?

I don't take fact finders any more and one of the main reasons is that I know the facts on just about everyone I meet, all the facts I need to start building a relationship. Let's take you. I know all the facts I need to know about you, and we've never met. See if I'm right .....

Do you like to be listened to?
Do you like to be loved?
Do you want me to hurt you?
Do you want to hurt me?

I hope you someday reach the stage in your career where you can build relationships without fact finders, without reading any more books. Until then, develop your own personal fact finder and use it. It'll help you build those close relationships so vital to a sale.

The Medical

People are fascinated with their bodies. This is why I always take customers in for the medical or meet them there.

I try to use the same doctor over and over again. He's only human and will appreciate your business and your professional manner and sincerity. When a customer has a blood pressure problem from being tense and uptight after a hard day at the plant or office, the doctor may give him (and you) a break by letting him calm down or take the exam another day.

When my customer and I arrive at the doctor's office I always greet the nurse warmly, yell "Hi" to the doc, and go over the requirements with the nurse, using medical jargon. "Okay, Sally, Mr. Customer is going to have a P & A. and a lateral. We want to get a good look at the heart position and size. Oh, and Sally, he'll need a double masters and be sure to have doc get that pulse rate up. This guy is a jogger and he might have some trouble ....."

You then sit down for a few minutes with your customer and explain your last remark, saying that his jogging has probably strengthened his heart which means it may take more stress to elevate his heart rate.

Now it's time for weigh in. You make him take off his shoes, empty his pockets, and if he has one of those big western belts with the giant buckles, that comes off too. I don't care if he's a string bean. He gets weighed with you watching attentively. Now you have him put his shoes back on and they take his height. You ask him to stand up real tall and you repeat the numbers that the nurse calls out.

He goes in to see the doc and you go right with him and sit through the questions. If anything unusual comes up you make sure a complete and clear explanation is given. Oh, yes -- before he goes in, make certain he knows about the stupid questions like "Do you ever have headaches .... chest pains?" "Have you ever consumed alcohol in excessive amounts?" Remind him that this is an insurance physical and while you don't want him to lie, there's no reason to convict himself .....

By being in on this all-important interview, you pick up all kinds of information. Most importantly you make certain that the home office underwriting team gets the right answers and complete ones.

While he's in taking the physical you fill out the application and have all the various forms for ulcer information, occupational hazards, and other papers ready to sign. After the medical is over you explain just exactly what blood pressure and heart rate mean. If he had to take a blood test (SMA 12) you whip out your paper explaining what each of the 12 tests are and what they hope to discover from them.

By the time you finish all this you are, in his mind, quite knowledgeable about one of the most important things in his life ... his body.

When you finish talking with him about blood pressure pull out the forms and point to the various places he needs to sign. There'll be no resistance ... not if you've done your job honestly, sincerely, and correctly.

The medical, in my mind, is one of the most important relationship-building areas in our business. Don't just send your customers over there ... go with them or meet them at the office. You may avoid a problem due to some mix-up with the nurse or doctor. Most importantly, your being there shows that you care.

Newsletters and Monthly Mailings

Don't buy tax service letters, financial reports, or your com-pany's monthly magazine with all the cute articles and then the pitch for insurance.

Save your money.

Write your own monthly newsletter. You may not think you have the skill to put out your own letter but you do if you're do-ing the things I've been telling you to do.

The purpose of the letter is public relations, to make you out as a unique individual with your own style. Here's what goes into my newsletter .....

I write up all new customers and introduce them to the other folks. Say I pick up a painting contractor. I talk about the business and how great the people are. Then I tell the rest of the gang to give them a call if they need non-union painting or want a good deal on wallpaper for their homes or offices.

If it's an individual, I describe that person's background and where he or she works ... just a few lines but they pump the customer up.

Next I might put in a "want ad" like a contractor has a pickup truck for sale ... how much and where to call. Sometimes I even put in a "help wanted" ad ... a contractor (unnamed) is looking for a top-flight superintendant for commercial shopping center construction.

Then I throw in advice on taxes or a tip that I heard or some such. Sometimes I cut out an interesting item from the newspaper and just tape it to the letter for copying as part of the mailout.

I also run year-end "sales" and "close-outs." I might say that I only have a few policies left for sale this month so you'd better call in quick and get one before they're gone. Stuff like that. They love it! It puts what I do "up front" and lets me be a real person with my customers.

This kind of stuff is interesting, original, and keeps your name in front of your people and lets them feel a part of your business. Try it! You'll have so much fun you may decide to go into the newspaper business!

Study Groups

In your own company and also within the MDRT, there are outstanding study groups that meet at least once a year.

You take your spouses. That's a must. They mingle with each other and share their stories while you study. You pay your own way. The group rents its own conference room or sets one couple up in a big suite and uses that as the conference room.

Mornings are for studying. Afternoons are for relaxing and relationship-building, usually with one other couple. Evenings are generally spent as a group going to a fine restaurant, ordering what you want, and then just splitting the bill regardless of what anyone orders. (Make certain that you talk this over before dinner so no one is irritated if someone orders imported wine. Or, have the booze put on separate checks.)

Your study group will help you form friendships that will last a lifetime. You'll get some great ideas that you'll use until they don't work any more. Year after year you'll look forward to being with these friends from all parts of the country, hearing how they have progressed or regressed, sharing tales .....

Most of all, you need to be with a group of people who have things in common and who are all together in their heads, at least on important things. It'll be a joy to be able to talk without relationship tension, to tell the truth about your production, to find that the sins of the others are just as bad and sometimes worse than your own, to feel, in a word, normal.

Then, sadly, most of the original members will just fade away after a few years. The group will disband or you won't go, but you'll retain those close friendships with one or two or three couples for the rest of your life.

Study groups are a must after you've been in the business at least two years. If you join before that, I doubt you'll feel comfortable. I doubt you'll even be invited, for that matter. But if you are, go and keep your mouth shut and your ears open ... and make friends.

What to Read and Study

Keep a copy of *Tax Facts* handy so if you get cancelled on an appointment or have to wait in the reception room you can read good stuff. Keep advanced underwriting memos from the home office in your jacket pocket for the same reason. Try to do any insurance-related reading while you're working.

At home, be certain to have the various trade magazines on your nightstand or in the bathroom so you can keep up to date with your customers' industry.

To stay well-rounded, read *Forbes*. It's the best magazine for giving you deep insight into various industries and the world. Force yourself to read every article. If you keep it in the bathroom you'll get the job done. You'll have plenty of high-interest information that you can discuss with your customers in business.

You just HAVE to be well-rounded in business information and world conditions. This makes you interesting and builds your relationships. People will begin to value your companionship because you can bring them up to date in their thinking and shore up their unfounded attitudes with facts and commentary that's fresh and well-written.

Time and time again I finish reading an article on some company or "tycoon" in *Forbes* and a few days later, the subject pops up. What a good feeling it is to be able to join the discussion with some solid background knowledge.

Sometimes you pick up a piece of information so valuable that you get on the phone immediately and call a customer. I remember reading that the United States was removing some restriction on beef and we'd soon be able to export more to Japan. The week before, a customer of mine had told me that he was thinking about going into cattle with a pal from Missouri. I called him, he checked out the story, and it helped him make the decision to go into the deal.

Don't waste time reading industry junk. Most of the articles I've read in life insurance magazines ... well, I just couldn't relate to them and I learned very little from them. Remember, you don't need to know much about life insurance once you know how the rate book works. Your home office is filled with "experts" who can fix anything you want fixed. You just sell life insurance. Concentrate on learning all you can about your customers' industry ... not the life insurance business.

Recommended Reading For You and Your Customers

First read these books yourself. Then start passing them out to customers and friends.

Yes, this is expensive. But considering what great sources of relationship-building conversation books are, the cost is nominal. Just stop sending those company mailouts and estate planning forms and so on ... and the birthday cards you don't even sign. Put the money into books. Better still, keep doing what you're doing and send books too! Remember, you don't have to invest in much ... put some bucks into your business like everyone else in business must do.

How to Read a Person Like a Book
By Gerard I. Nierenberr and Henry H. Calero, Published by Pocket Book #78593

Body Language
By Julius Fast, Published by M. Evans and Co.

The Time Trap
By Alex Mackenzie, Published by McGraw Hill

The Lushcher Color Test
By Ian Scott, Published by Pocket Book #78827

Type "A" Behavior and Your Heart
By Dr. Meyer Friedman, Published by Alfred A. Knopf

Body, Mind and Sugar
By Emanuel Maurice Abrahamson, Published by Holt, Rinehart

Widow
By Lynn Caine, Published by William Morrow

So What Are You Going To Do Now?

You've read this book. That means you probably think about the same way I do. So, you had some laughs as I took a poke at management, home office people, record keeping, CLU, meetings, contests, prospecting, and just about everything held near and dear by the "establishment."

But don't laugh too hard or too long, my friend. They've been here for 150 years plus ... and will be here long after you and I have put down the pen and application.

The point is that the material in this book is meant for your PRIVATE use and shouldn't be used to bang the establishment over the head. You'll be asking for all kinds of trouble if you do.

Take a long walk in a park or field somewhere. Clear your mind of all that you know. Dare to think how you'd really like to work and live and what kind of money you want in your pocket. Forget about the business for a moment. Just think about you.

Okay. What's standing in the way of your dreams? That's right: death and disability. Did you get that cleared up? Did you already get your will and trust drawn? Written the letters to your family about every detail of your funeral, your estate? Letters to clients and friends? Selected and communicated to the agent who'll take over your client files?

You've done all that? Fine. Now go in and clean up your desk. Throw away all the articles you want to read, all the home office material. Cancel all meetings, every one except MDRT. Get your cassette player in the car and your MDRT tapes and Feldmen's tapes and my two from '74 and '77. Got your *Tax Facts*? Told your family you don't watch TV any more? Good!

Now pick out the industry you want to work in and go call on some people. No more prospecting ... no more guilty feeling when you don't put the local super market manager through a "funnel" and put him on one of those stupid cards ... no more white, green, and pink cards ... no more distractions. Just find out what someone is afraid of, who they love, and who'll be hurt if they die ... and write the business.

Term? Fine. Make them a customer. Whole life? Fine. Write it up. Be a salesperson, "just" a salesperson. You now have the tools ... use them.

Appendix: A Couple of Related Pieces

The following articles are reprinted, with permission, from the Million Dollar Round Table *Proceedings*.

The Businessman—Is He Really A Big Bad Wolf?

Kent P. Larsen

In the early days of the Roman Empire, the marketplace was filled with statues carved of marble quarried from the nearby hills. The ones that had flaws were filled with wax and had to be kept in the shadows. They could not stand the heat of the brilliant Roman sunlight.

My words will be held to the sunlight of your experience. They will be tested by the power of your minds. They will not melt. They will meet that test and you will know that I am not filled with wax.

The gift I have for you is wrapped in honest sweat and toil. I want to hand you the heart of a lion. I want you to feel it pulsate. I want you to capture the power, the energy, the love that exists in the heart of the American businessman. He's just down the street and up the block. No, not on the golf course or in the local bar. He is pacing his office, sleeves rolled up, tie undone. There is a twinkle in his eye and fire in his guts. He is waiting for you. He is the American businessman.

But you don't knock on his door. You don't hand him aspirin to relieve the fire. Oh, I know. You tried to see him and he looked at you like some slimy creature from the bottomless pit. So you left him where he usually can be found . . . ALONE. ALL ALONE.

So now you busy yourself. And the life insurance industry wonders why such a small percentage of its business is written from the business insurance cases. The industry and your company in particular all would like to know why the businessman is so hard to reach. Why is he such a "hard sell?" Why are so few agents able to meet the standards and fill the bill?

On these pages you will find out the answer. The problem, simply stated, is that you are all too busy studying how chickens lay eggs. That's right, call it CLU, advanced underwriting, or whatever, but it all boils down to studying how chickens lay eggs. You read books about that chicken. You diagram the "big bird" and may even have put your eyes and nose tight down there to watch the whole process. You can study, you can read and you can observe how a chicken lays an egg but if you are not a chicken, YOU WILL NEVER KNOW THE SENSATION!

That's the part not found in the books or the lectures. The sensation. The sensation of doing business. You can't understand the businessman until you have felt his pain, suffered a little of his agony, been on his side of the desk fighting the battle, making a decision every minute while weighing what not to do rather than what to do for fear he may be working on a low priority task and blowing a big one.

Here is his day. Here are his inner thoughts. Here is an in-depth, fact finding interview that touches deep into his soul. Come with me now, crawl inside his brain and into one of his days.

Come with me. I want to try and give you the "sensation of business," the "feel" for the man you want so very much to work with, the sensation of the agony and the ecstasy of building an American business.

The day doesn't start at any particular time. A month is a moment, and a year is a blur. There is no identity with just one day. Because we must begin somewhere, we might as well pick the middle of the night.

He has been tossing and turning, fighting for sleep because he knows he must get some to keep from screaming at his people if his nerves are raw. And then, he looks up at the ceiling in his bedroom where his God usually looks down at him and he utters, "Lord, if tomorrow is going to be anything like today . . . take me now . . . I'm ready to go!" Death would be a release, especially if he is in the black on the financial statement.

Finally, in the early morning hours sheer fatigue brings blessed relief, relief he may have tried to force with a few drinks at dinner. Sometimes he wishes he could take his brain out of his head and put it in an ice bucket just to cool the damn thing off.

Sleep comes at last, until he is shattered back to consciousness by the ring of the small alarm hidden under his pillow, shattered awareness that his darlin' wife will be disturbed at too early an hour if he doesn't silence that ring. She softly questions, "Honey, what time is it?" "Oh, about six," he lies. "It is not," she screams, "it's probably about five. You're stupid! Why don't you just stay down at that place where you flap your mouth all day!"

You don't scream back. You are stupid! You're the boss. Then why the devil are you going down there at this hour? The people won't be in for hours. You are stupid, so you don't say anything.

You wouldn't dare ask her to fix your breakfast, so you wander downstairs and fix yourself a bowl of munchy crunchies and some horrible instant coffee. You fill up with vitamins because some man told you it would keep your temper in check and calm your nerves and give you more energy at night so you could be a "better companion" to that little darlin' wife, even though you are wiped out and ready to try for some sleep by 9:00 p.m.

You put on your coat, tiptoe in to give your children a silent, secret kiss, tell yourself that they are so beautiful—like little angels—and that this Saturday you are GOING TO BE WITH THEM . . . BODY, MIND AND SPIRIT and that lousy business can go to hell!

You open the front door and step outside into the morning air. The miracle happens: you are transfigured! The feel of that morning air brings out the eternal optimism of the American businessman. Once outside, he enters the jungle and he is the King of Beasts, the Lion of Men, capable of taking everything life offers as a challenge. Gone is yesterday, he is a free man, he is in control, he can change, rebuild, fight a new day through and come out on top.

He pulls up in front of his office, his shop or his warehouse. Out comes the key, a piece of pot metal worth a penny. It slips into a lock on the door. It could be a little door, a skinny door, a fat door, a big door. It doesn't matter, it's HIS DOOR; and that key, that's HIS KEY to HIS DOOR.

He walks in. It could be an old dusty warehouse, half filled with litter, but to him it's his Taj Mahal. It's not what anyone else sees, it's what is going to be there, what it will be, and to him it's utterly beautiful and breathtaking. He never tires just walking out there, even alone. He knows that he knows and one day EVERYONE else will know too.

But, it's time for action—the beginning of a new day and he must perform "the ritual."

If you unbutton the shirt of the American businessman, you will find a small, neat zipper in his chest. He walks over to his desk, unzips the zipper and takes his heart out, lays it down on the desk, reaches over for a special kind of club and starts beating his heart until it is a bloody mass of pulsating flesh. He scoops it up, puts it back into his chest, zips up the zipper, buttons his shirt, prepares for the day and slips out into the shops to greet his "troops" with a "Hey! Good morning! How's it going? Let's give 'em hell today."

This ritual is performed so that there is no pain left to be felt as he suffers the slings and arrows of his own personal failings and the failings of those he needs most, no pain left to feel when he finds the hours unfolding and pressure building as he is stretched taut by problems never totally solvable.

At about 9:00 a.m. Joe Salesmanager walks in and says, "I've had it! I'm leavin' and I'm happy to leave you and this rotten company!" "Now, Joe," he says, "take it easy. Look, let's have lunch and talk this problem out. If we can talk, Joe, we can make a good deal for both of us." So, a lunch appointment is quickly cancelled and Joe Salesmanager is plugged in. It isn't that he is worried about losing Joe, it's just that he knows what he's got. But what might be next? And, he doesn't want to do his job and Joe's until he finds another body to take his place.

At 11:00 a.m. the banker calls. He wants money! Now! Why? You are overdrawn and you have gone above and beyond your credit line time and time again. Now the banker wants his money and he wants a deposit to cover the overdrafts by 3:00 p.m. that day. No excuses. No more promises. Just get the money there or the payroll bounces.

You never let a payroll bounce. The guys in the shipping room have trouble with zip codes and counting the right number of boxes on an order, but let their paycheck be short three cents and they spot it like an IBM computer and storm into Payroll with blood in their eyes. You never let a payroll check bounce. NEVER!

So, you call in the sweet young thing that handles Accounts Receivable and you tell her the good news. You need $11,000 by 3:00 p.m. today and you want her to give you a list of the customers who owe money. She does instantly, but hands you only one name. That's all, just one name—George Slowpay. You call George Slowpay and say, "Hi, George! How's it going?" You don't particularly like George. He is slow paying and curses over any petty item not perfect and then makes you sweat it out for payment six months with the threat of a big order just around the corner. You don't have too much of a choice whom you deal with. You have a market, the market has customers and you deal with them as best you can or get out of the market. It's just that simple.

"George, I need $11,000 of the $23,000 you've owed us for five months." "What?" screams George through the phone. "Look, I told you guys a million times, when we get paid you get paid, and we ain't been paid yet!" "But, George, I just have to have it or I am really in trouble." "Well," says George, "if we are going to be in the finance business as well as be one of your biggest customers . . ."

Now you're getting hot—not too hot though because your back is up against the wall. You never heard of unencumbered capital. You don't have any "quiet money" laying in reserve. You're a "good money manager" and have every dime out working as hard as it will run for every point of profit it can make.

You hang in there with George Slowpay. "Look, George, how much do you want for $11,000?" "Well," he says, "send me over an invoice for $12,000 and I'll give you the $11,000." You say, "Thank you George. Gee, I really appreciate it, George," (you S.O.B.). And you send over the invoice discounting your bill $1,000 so that your doors can stay open.

Sometimes I wonder about advanced underwriters who are so impressed with their ledger sheets and figures arguing about buy term and invest the difference and playing their little silly games with 1 percent and 3 percent.

Cash is the king! Credit is the queen. Unencumbered capital means the difference between survival or failure. Reserve cash can be doubled in 10 minutes. What kind of a percentage is that all you great brainy agents with your minimum deposit insurance?

How does a businessman get cash? He hides it—most of all from himself. He plays games like "Put $500 a month into dumb life insurance," and one day he will have a pile of "quiet money" and he won't have to crawl on his knees to a jerk like George Slowpay. And he can have his manhood back by being able to tell him to forget the next big order.

That's what unencumbered cash reserves are. Burn that into all your brains, fellow insurance agents!

To get back to "The Day." Well, after solving the payoff crisis, he now meets Joe

Salesmanager for lunch. He slaps him on the back, lies a little and gives him a $200 a month raise. He buys his body, he buys meat, Grade A meat. He is in the "People Business," not the construction business, not the engineering business, not the manufacturing business, but the "People Business."

And he is buying without one of the greatest financial tools ever conceived: nonqualified, unfunded, forfeitable, deferred compensation. He never even heard of this miracle. Why? Because he won't talk to you, he won't give you more than five minutes, he cuts himself off from someone who could bring him aspirin to relieve the pain—a new weapon for his private arsenal.

At 2:00 p.m. his little darlin' wife calls to remind him to be home early. "Be home at five this evening. Remember, it's Sally Sue's birthday and you have to play the clown." "Yes, honey, I'll be home, I'll be there, yes, I know I've said that before. Who is more important than you guys? I'LL BE THERE. Goodbye, honey."

At 3:00 p.m. the biggest potential customer in the company's history is on the phone long distance. He tells you that your contract has been approved this morning by their board of directors and recommends that you catch a plane and meet him for dinner to sign the agreements.

You call the airport. Guess what time the last plane leaves? Of course, 5:00 o'clock!

So, you make that miserable phone call. Two words aren't out of your mouth when she hangs up on you. You dial back; cold silence greets you. "But, honey," you say, "I have to go." "You mean there isn't anyone else in that entire company who can go besides you? Don't tell me that nonsense! What kind of a manager are you? Do you have to do everything yourself? What do you pay all those people for anyhow?"

You try to explain, you're torn apart, you have a responsibility. How can you put together the words to tell her that you really care, that playing the clown is really important, more important than she will ever know, but you can't. You hang up. There is an empty feeling inside. You wonder if all this is worth it. A few minutes go by; that's all the time you are allowed for your personal agony.

Rosey, your secretary, comes in and places a small white card on your desk. She tells you that Mr. Agent from Podunk Life is just outside and would like 10 minutes of your time to show you an idea proven valuable to companies like yours.

"Rosey, tell him I have an idea for him too. What are we, a refuge for every damn insurance agent that walks the street? That's the fifth one this week! Didn't I tell you to screen my calls? Tell the guy he has five lousy minutes."

In walks Mr. Agent. You hate him instantly. Sweet smelling, clean, pressed and neat, full of enthusiasm and just bubbling. That in itself is enough to drive this harried businessman up the wall.

The businessman is a salesman himself. He has to be. He sells his family, his employees, his creditors, and his customers. "Look," he says, "you are wasting your time and mine. I am blued and tatooed with enough damn insurance to paper the walls with the policies. We have had Neighbor John for our personal and corporate agent for the last 10 years. He loves me and I am totally in love with him. My accountant tells me that must be the reason we pay so damn much in premiums each year. So, why not have a cup of coffee out in the lobby and go down the street and find some new business or something?"

If the agent starts to pitter-patter countering the objections because he has been told by his supervisor just how to have an answer for everything, well, he could be physically ejected. After all, insurance agents are not the only people who read sales books!

The agent leaves. Out of the door he goes, and never comes back. He walks out into the street, gets into the car and wonders how anyone so crude and ignorant could run a large business.

The agent did not have a feeling for business. He had been busy studying how chickens lay eggs instead of trying to capture the sensation. He couldn't look at the businessman with the thing that man needed most: kind, understanding, compassionate eyes. He couldn't say to him, "Look, I know how you bleed inside, buddy, how raw you are rubbed in so many places. I'm not here to hurt you, I am here to help you. I have answers to serious problems that will ease your pain. If you knew what I knew you would jump up and down in the middle of that workloaded desk. You don't want to see me now, but I'll come back—again and again until you somehow realize that I am here to help you."

And come back. You may be the only friend he can have. It is so lonely, so utterly lonely. Who can the businessman really talk to? His wife? No. She has problems of her own and probably views the business more as a threat than an ally. She sees how it tears her husband up, down and sideways when he vents his frustration on her and the children, and later she finds him softly crying in silence while checking the little ones when they are fast asleep.

Can he talk with his suppliers? No. One day their prices may jump, and he doesn't want to know that he is cutting off Sam and Mary. His employees? No. One day he might have to put his foot in the middle of Hank's back and shove him out the door and he doesn't want to know about the impact it would have on Hank's family. That's right, our businessman is a softy; he hurts when you pinch and bleeds when you cut.

And so he sits there in that chair day after day with no one to really talk to who understands and can bring him something that will raise his self-esteem, give him some hope that it won't always be this way, that there is more to a business than the occasional hilarity and joy that comes with a big contract or a beautiful black figure on the bottom of the quarterly financial statement.

Our business man readies himself for the trip out of town. He walks into the shop and tells his partner and production manager the exciting news about the new contract. Inside he is torn apart over his family problem, but he keeps it from "Partner John."

John isn't as strong as he used to be when they first started business. He seems to have aged and lost the "zip," he doesn't get too excited over expansion anymore. He is more interested in building a cabin on that lot in Oregon where he hopes one day to retire.

You don't bother "Partner John" too much any more with details. You don't socialize with the families because you both learned long ago to keep your wives away from each other. You have witnessed what happened many times when a wife starts telling how hard her husband is working in front of the partner's wife, who probably hears a different story and has one of her own to tell.

No, you and John are dear friends but you have begun to outgrow him mentally. You wonder how you are going to move him out gently. You wouldn't hurt him for the world. It's just that you are getting tired of carrying him and sharing the profits from your brainwork too. You have some insurance to buy him out if he dies, but you don't even want to think about that.

Well, after you let John in on the news, you drive to the airport and the ugly thought of that plane falling down creeps into your mind. "Damn it! I should have a will. Well, when I get back this time . . ." You also wonder just how far John would get without you. He'd probably want to liquidate the company. Liquidate. Imagine! After all this, just when it looks so promising.

And then you have secret hopes that your son Paul will one day join you as you have seen other sons of men you admire join them. Liquidate. "Oh well, I'll be in a box, so who cares!"

You board the plane, meet with the customer, stroke him and he strokes you. You fly back that night and enter a darkened house. No sweet thing to greet you with a smile. No, she's exhausted from running the birthday party with 30 children all by herself. She's asleep. You tiptoe in and set that secret alarm. You fight for sleep that doesn't come. You look up at the ceiling for God. "If tomorrow is going to be anything like today, Lord, take me now!!!"

This, my fellow agents, is the "Sensation of Business."

Help this man. Help him. Forget about insurance. Help him get a will and a trust. Make the appointment for him with an attorney. Drive him over. Remake the appointment when he cancels a few times. Show him you care. Forget the insurance. Help him to understand the basics of business continuation and estate planning by explaining in his language, not insurance language. Get him prepared for the attorney so he won't feel like a dummy and not want to go. Forget the insurance.

Build him a dream. Show him corporate recapitalization that will move his aging partner out without destroying the capital of the company and its credit lines. Give him deferred compensation so that he can buy men with dollars that have meaning and make it painful for them to leave him for a few hundred more a month.

Give him a plan to take home to his wife. One that shows her it isn't all paper and talk, one that shows where one day the pressure can be lessened and that her children will have a company to run and not just a chance for a job.

Forget the insurance.

One day he will see that insurance is the glue and the fiber that will keep all these things together if he doesn't have time. He will ask you, you won't have to ask. He will sweat out the results of the medicals and call you for answers, you won't have to call him.

Help him. Forget about insurance. He will buy it, you never will sell it to him.

Are you strong enough for all this? Do you honestly care enough? Can you really think about him and his problems and forget yours? Can you be that someone he can talk to who understands? Can you be humble when he is being arrogant to cover his fears? Can you see through the veneer into his heart? Can you walk on his level, share his dreams, match his courage? God bless you if you can. If you can't, then stay away. Don't add to the parade of agents who pass through his doors day after day and force him to condemn those he never met and needs most of all.

You are moved by my words, I can tell. I can feel it . . . . . you understand . . . . . you relate . . . . . we are together now, you and I . . . . . and our friend, the American Businessman.

Ray Triplett, in this very same city a few years ago, told us that our business was 90 percent art and 10 percent science and that each of us were artists in every sense of the word. Michelangelo, perhaps one of the greatest artists and sculptors the world has ever known, was once asked to define his job, to explain just exactly what a sculptor does. He simply replied, "A sculptor is in the business of taking away . . . . . of taking away. . . . ."

Can't we just see him now, alone in his studio with a huge slab of marble just brought in, dirty, cracked and full of grime. We can picture him standing there looking INTO it and seeing. . . . . .DAVID . . . . .the PIETA! He would pick up his hammer and chisel and begin to take away . . . . . to take away.

And that is our job. We, too, are in the business of taking away. Tearing off the veener and breaking through the communication barriers to expose the businessman as he really is . . . . a wonderful, courageous and loving creature. And what are your tools? Are they the hammer and chisel? Oh no. . . . . . . you will use the tools of compassion, tenderness, understanding, empathy and LOVE.

And one day when you are finished with your work you will be able to put your arm around your work of art, the businessman, your friend and proclaim for all the world to hear . . . . SINCERE . . . . . SINCERE . . . . this statue has no wax!

Just A Salesman

Kent P. Larsen
and
David H. James, CLU

Each day, all over this world, people are objecting to our products. It's the same objections we hear day after day, over and over.

I want to talk it over with my wife. Now Charlie, if you are going to buy her some flowers, would you pick up the phone and call her and say, "Honey, what kind do you want?" No. You go out and buy some. You bring them home to her because you want to make her happy. And you want to love her a little. Now you see, Charlie, you've forgotten what we were doing. We're writing a love letter. You don't want her to help you write a love letter, that's my job. Let me help you write it.

I want some time to think it over. Time, you want me to give you time? I can't give you any time. Only God can give you time. All I can do is sell it to you. Write out a little check, buy a little time. Write out a bigger check, buy a big slice of time. But oh, please, don't ask me to *give* you time, because all I can do is sell it to you.

Let's get together next month. Next month, next year. What gives you the audacity to presume that you're going to be here *tomorrow?* Your heart beats from second to second. Tell you what, you call me just before you're going to die. I'll run. I'll wait. I'll go through life if we can get a single brain wave. If we can get you to steam up the glass. If you can lift that trembling hand and scratch your name on that piece of paper, I'll search the world. I'll get it. But it might be too late. You say, "Don't back up the hearse. Don't make me smell the flowers" You want an appointment next month. Before I take out my calendar and we pick a time, a day and a place, let me ask you a question, Charlie. When I call on that time, that day and that place, if you're not here, who shall I ask for? (And then be very quiet, because you never know what could happen next.)

I don't have any money. You don't have any money, I don't have any money, they don't have any money. Where the hell is all the money? You big dummy, that's why we're here! You don't have any money. So, all we're going to do is open up a line of credit at a different kind of a bank. Now, to keep that line open you have to pay a little teeny-weeny, little bit of interest. If you don't need to use the line we give your interest back. Now what's so hard about that?

What is this going to cost me? The first year's premium. Charlie, everybody knows that after you pay the first year's premium to a quality company, the policy is yours forever. Forever! Because anything you put in after that, you get back.

Once in awhile put away the 15-page proposals and 13-column ledger statements and just try that. It might work. But if he still pushes you in the corner and he's one of those numbers guys, he says, "That sounds pretty good. I like to see some numbers with a proposal, you know." I'll say, "Can I ask you a question? Are you looking for an excuse to say no? If you are, tell me now because I'll bring in a whole damn pickup truck full of numbers. We'll stack numbers up to the ceiling. We'll have proposals all over the place. And you know what's going to happen? It's going to cost $2,000 a year if you want to own it and $500 if you want to rent it. And it's going to be the price you pay for loving somebody. Now what's so hard about that?"

We talk to one man at a time. We're competing with Walter Kronkrite and the problems of his death. We need some exciting concepts and ideas to shake him, for his own good. So, I've invited a friend of mine, David James, a businessman, to come and help us with some concepts. David owns a very fine company. I've been introduced to David by his friend Pete. We have just toured his plant, and David very carefully has shown me every tool, how clean the bathrooms are, his landscaped yard in front of the building, the giant flag pole with the silver eagle. We have just come into his office, and we're now going to sit down and go to work.

"Dave, one of the reasons I like to get with you guys is because while we were walking through that shop, I got to know you. I don't know a thing about all those things you were showing me, but I do know about people. I was watching your face. You thrilled me, to see the gleam and the sparkle in your eye. You're proud of that bunch of characters out there, aren't you? That's why those aisles and toilets are clean and the mirrors scrubbed.

"Pete sent me here because he was a little bit afraid for you. We're not going to talk about insurance and all that stuff. That's not what I'm here for. I want to talk about your wife, Carol. I'm talking about Carol going shopping, it's Friday and she's got the groceries in the back of the station wagon. Her mind's preoccupied, she's hurrying home to fix dinner for you. She's driving along that freeway, not paying much attention, and suddenly out of nowhere, a hippie high on marijuana, driving an old Volkswagen bus with the American flag draped all around the windows, moves her over into a concrete caison. Now she's 118 pounds of goo on the freeway. That would be pretty tragic.

"I know businessmen whom that's happened to. Another tragedy that's just as painful is when a few months later you find your doors locked and you're going to have to buy your business back from the government."

We don't have to go any further. You can take it from there. The point I want to make is that we didn't talk about a lot of facts and figures. All we did was kill his wife and destroy his business.

Now I'll give you the concept that never fails to get prospects excited. It's called the "superstar contract." It goes something like this.

"As you know, the Cincinnati Reds have Pete and they have Little Joe, and they got Johnny back there. And oh Willie Joe Namath is going to drop those big bombs in L.A. for us this year. You know what those guys are? They're *superstars*. But you've got a shop out there, a profitable shop. I saw the numbers. And you've got superstars working there, whether it's the production manager or the guy on the loading dock. They're superstars. You know what would be exciting? To wack a zero off a Catfish Hunter's contract. Get it down to our size and lay one up on them. You know why? Because they aren't afraid of you any more. They can walk down the street and get another job. In fact you're afraid of them now. When you walk by there's no quivering and shaking because the boss is coming. He'll just say, "Who in the hell is that guy?" Isn't that right?

"How would you like to have him pucker a little bit? How would you like to be the White Knight out in that shop? I'll tell you you lay 250 big ones on that production superintendent, he'll give you a flick when you walk by. Or here's something even more exciting. I've got some lessons for your arsenal of negotiation. I've got new things for you—good ideas. You know, you need *people*. You can get capital, go to the bank, find it, steal it, scratch it somewhere, but you can't get people. Only the flakes are walking the streets. Only the flakes are banging on the doors. The good guys are tight, they're in there working aren't they?

"How would you like to pick up your phone, call your competitor's best man, the guy you've known and watched for years but he won't leave. How would you like to pick up the phone and say, 'Hey, George, come on over. I want to have lunch with you and I want to offer you $250,000. A quarter of a million up front if you'll just sit down. I want you to be my superstar, George.' How would that feel?

"But now, just to make sure that I get this point across to you, $250,000 may be a lot of money, but I like to really have it hit you hard. No point in being insulted, I'm not trying to get your wrath. But this is a very good company. What if IBM or Xerox or Transamerica suddenly decides to go into widgets and you got a phone call from the senior vice president of IBM. 'Mr. James, we'd like to have lunch. We'd like to buy your company, and for starters we'd like to give you a million dollar contract up front.' Do you think he'd have lunch? You're right."

Well, you can take it from there. That's just cellophane gift wrapped deferred comp. That's all it is.

Now, we can't really have anybody die and come back. We can sure as heck have them feel the impact of being disabled. Here's something very powerful. You have to be careful because you can put somebody into the looney house with it. This is tough stuff. You're going to all participate in this. You're going to feel the panic. We're going to talk about being *disabled*. Let's see if we can have a prospect feel the sensation of being disabled. Why don't we have him stick his fingers in his ears just for a minute.

"David, that's pretty tough to go around like that. But it would be a heck of a lot worse if you didn't have any money. But, you know, Dave, you could overcome that, but we're only a sixteenth of an inch away from being in a basket. You've got little hunks of nerves running down the middle of your back called the spinal cord. It holds everything and its only about a sixteenth of an inch thick. If you suffered the right blow on the back of the head and this cord snapped, you'd be a bubbling banana.

"Now, what I want you to do, David, is to feel the sheer hopelessness and terror of the real world. I can't take you along with me when I deliver the death checks and visit the hospitals with the disability checks, so I want to invite you into this world with me. I want you now to just freeze. Don't move an inch. You're totally paralyzed. You can only move your eyelids, blink once for a yes, twice for a no while I ask you some questions. 'David, how are you feeling today? Oh, gee, forgive me. Would you like some breakfast? How about some eggs? Over easy? Scrambled? Some orange juice? How about some tomato juice? Tomato juice. Can I get you anything else? I'm such a klutz, Dave, I'm sorry. Would that be all you wanted? It's not all you want?' OK. Alright, that's good."

David has now lost his manufacturing company and he's CPA, an attorney, manufacturers rep, a salesman.

"David, you and I have some of the same problems. When you stop, everything stops. When I stop, everything stops. I'm sure you've had many salesmen approach you with the idea of buying some disability insurance, and so forth. And you've said, 'That's not a very exciting thing, you know, laying out all that money for something that might not happen.' So instead of asking you to do that, today I'd like you to buy a lease with an option to buy on a manufacturing building. That way you can have some income if that sixteenth of an inch snapped or that delicate hearing goes. I'd like you to consider leasing a manufacturing building with an option to buy. And if anything like that ever happens, suddenly you will have 30 men out there pulling machines. You'll have the best superintendent in town. You'll have the finest manufacturing company ever conceived by man, and every profit will be tax-free. We're talking about a million dollars! A million-dollar manufacturing company. Along with this manufacturing company—for free, with no extra cost because I know you don't like life insurance—we'll throw in $1 million of life insurance. Would you like me to tell you about that building?"

I can't get excited about the regular disability policy because to most of my clients $3,000 a month won't even make their house payments. Let's talk about a marvelous product called yearly renewable term, which would be sold by a company that, when you add waiver of premium to the term and a guy becomes disabled, a few companies will allow you to convert that term to whole life, and they will pay the whole life premium. That means a guy, say, 40, for around $400 can buy $100,000 worth of disability. Or for $4,000 can buy $1,200,000 because that's what the cash values would accumulate to. Now you're talking about selling a million dollar disability package for $4,000 and you throw in life insurance for free! That just goes along with the package. And to the corporation guy, you can *double it* and sell him $2 million. That's how I like to move disability. I like to work with big numbers and get people excited about it.

While we've been talking, sharing ideas and concepts, there's been a whole unseen world around us. It's a world in which so many of you are blind to, which we hope to open your eyes a little bit, keep your curiosity and get you to look into these worlds. There's a whole world of non-verbal communication and part of that world is *color*. Color has impact as a communication vehicle. Let's see if we can *feel* color and what it might mean.

Let's try *red*. Can't you feel that naked aggression? That achievement? That oversexed drive of *red?* Watch out for the guy who drives that red car with the white interior. Drives all over town. Red-Red-Red! Watch out for him—he's an aggressive, achievement-oriented individual and he might roll over you.

What about the *browns?* The ambers? Ah, it just makes you feel *secure*. Brown. Brown car. Saddle interior. Brown suit, brown tie, brown furniture, Brown-Brown-*Brownie!* What's a brownie? I'm a brownie. Do you know why? People who are most attracted to brown are usually concerned that they don't have as much control over their situation as they'd like. So, they go to brown because it's a *security* color. It makes them feel good. It makes them feel secure.

Now, what about the healthy color *blue?* What a wonderful color, *blue*. A blue car. Blue suit. Blue-Blue-Blue-*Bluey!* Blue people are marvelous, healthy people. They can be in the thick of things, with confrontations, antagonism all around them, but they're attracted to blue because deep down they don't want confrontation. They love things to go smooth. They like *serenity*. So much for color.

There's another theory of our work which you've read some books on, and it really works. It really means something. It's the world of *body language*, communication. David is going to be that businessman. If we know and understand what this is about we can tell something about ourselves and about him and how things are going. He's crying out to tell you how he really feels. Not everybody can just tell you how they feel. They hide it, but their bodies show it. Here's how it's done.

Now David's leaning forward. He's in an aggressive, controlling posture. He starts talking with his fingers; tapping his fingers, squirming around, looking around. He said, "Let's get this action going. Come on, you're not doing anything. Come on, let's go, *do something*. I'm bored."

What about taking his glasses off and rubbing his eyes? He'll probably say something like, "Well Larsen, yeah, that's a pretty good idea." But what he's really saying is, "I can't see it. You're a pain in the neck!"

Now he is putting his glasses back on. Oh, I've antagonized him. He folded his hands, folded his arms, turned his shoulder to me, ankles locked. Now, look, when you take a prospect out to a restaurant for lunch, drop the napkin on the floor and look to see if his ankles are locked. If they're locked, he's a little uncomfortable. Get those feet apart! You'll feel better, you'll act better, your body will tell you everything's OK. You've got to get him out of that position. How are we going to do it? Ask him something—anything about nothing!

Now, oh such an important gesture. Any time someone puts his hands to his lips while your talking, you might as well forget about continuing because the judicious thought process is going on. He's thinking about something you've said. If, when you saw that hand go up, you just stopped, he wouldn't even notice that you've stopped. He'll just start talking, especially if he cocks his head at the same time.

Selling is a lot of fun, but not always. You know that. Sometimes it seems like there's 100,000 people lined up in front of you as if forming a wall. They are good, well-intentioned but nonetheless ignorant people. Who are these critics? Sometimes they are an attorney, sometimes a CPA. He says, "Get out of here. How dare you call on my client. How dare you tell me what should be done. You're nothing but a salesman. A crummy, commission-hungry merchant of doom. Go away!" They can hurt you. They can tear your guts out. They can rip you apart, make you depressed.

But, who stands and looks at the wounded earth that's just been opened at a gravesite? Who stands next to a not-so-young girl with silver in her hair, shuddering, practically sobbing, knowing that he won't be home ever again? All the battles they fought together are over forever. Who is it who walks over, takes her in his arms and says, "Mary, it's going to be lonely. Mary, it will be OK. You'll never be poor." Who does that? *The salesman!*

Who goes over and takes a big hunk of a man, shaken, ripped apart, bewildered, confused over the death of a partner of 20 years? Who takes that man by the warehouse door, saying, "Bill, take out the keys. Open the door, Bill. There's a hundred people waiting for you. Bill, it's OK. You're going to make it. We'll all miss him. Bill come on, we need you. Turn the key. Forget about the rest. I'll take care of that. It's all taken care of. We did all that. It's going to be OK. Who does that? *Just a salesman!*

When you go back to your homes, your cities, towns and farmlands, stay out of your office. Go and be with the people. Open your heart. Pour out your heart. And be so proud, forever, of being just a salesman.